Glen Aubrey
www.glenaubrey.com

2012 Emmy® Award Winning Songwriter and Arranger
National Academy of Television Arts & Sciences
Pacific Southwest Chapter
Thirty-eighth Annual Pacific Southwest Emmy® Awards

Author:
Leadership Is—How to Build Your Legacy
Industrial Strength Solutions Build Successful Work Teams!
Core Teams Work Their Principles and Practices
L.E.A.D.—Learning, Education, Action, Destiny
Leadership Works—Advanced Study Guide for L.E.A.D.
Lincoln, Leadership and Gettysburg—Defining Moments of Greatness
Go From the Night—Journeys of Thought, Meditations on Life
Freedom Light—Expressions of Hope and Evidence
Lessons of War—Lincoln's Second Inaugural Address, Leadership at Gettysburg
Lincoln's Leadership—If You Want Success, Lead Like This
Permission—Sharing Relational Opportunity, The Essence of Respectful and Gracious Interaction

Endorsements on behalf of Glen Aubrey

Books and Professional Consultation Services
Creative Team Resources Group (CTRG)
www.ctrg.com

Cal Thomas, Syndicated Columnist,
Fox News Contributor
Core Teams Work

"There are two roads to business and personal success. One pursues success as an end in itself, often poisoning relationships and corrupting morals; the other road is paved with sound and proven principles which succeed without poisoning relationships and without the guilt. Glen Aubrey shows us how to succeed in business and in life by taking the second and better road."

Malcolm Dougherty, Director, California Department of Transportation (Caltrans)
Core Teams Work

"As a leader in a large organization I realize my executive managers are experts and leaders in their own right, but it is my job to ensure they function as an efficient, high performing team. *Core Teams Work* explores the dynamics of teamwork that can either help or hinder the entire organization's performance…"

Seth Godin, Author, *Purple Cow*
Industrial Strength Solutions
"No fancy theories here, just the realities of working with (and leading) teams. This book will make you think—hard—about what it means to lead."

Major General Robert F. Dees, United States Army, Retired
Lessons of War—Lincoln's Second Inaugural Address, Leadership at Gettysburg
"*Lessons of War—Lincoln's Second Inaugural Address, Leadership at Gettysburg* is a tremendous contribution to the art and science of strategic leadership, as viewed through the crucible of human conflict. Glen Aubrey's insightful reflections into President Lincoln's Second Inaugural Address, particularly how Abraham Lincoln 'set the conditions' for our nation's fateful transition from civil war to lasting peace, is critically relevant to the daunting challenges faced by our current senior political and military leaders, as they also determine how best to turn swords into plowshares in Iraq, Afghanistan, and beyond."

Kevin D. Bouren, Major, U.S. Army, Executive Officer, Directorate of Admissions
United States Military Academy at West Point
Lessons of War—Lincoln's Second Inaugural Address, Leadership at Gettysburg
"With his clear and engaging style, Glen once again delivers a fascinating and indispensable examination of leadership, this time through the lens of an American hero. Lincoln's powerful legacy of strong leadership in war, founded upon his reverence for God, is a sterling model for every leader. Military and civilian leaders must apply the timeless lessons gleaned from

Glen's analysis, particularly during this age of enduring conflict."

"The Directorate of Admissions at West Point is proud to endorse Glen Aubrey and the CTRG organization, and the great work they have done for us... One element that has truly had a profound impact on our team was the formulation of our Values, Vision, Mission, and Message. After ratifying this document as a team, it is now used to measure our performance across a broad range of activities. Our Core Values have also helped us to screen potential employees to determine if they are the right fit for us as they determine if we are the right fit for them. Invaluable.

"Glen Aubrey is a tremendous facilitator, mentor, leader, and team-builder. We are greatly indebted to him and CTRG for their timely recommendations and priceless input to our team. Without a doubt, we will go farther and do better now that we have partnered with Glen's incredible team of professionals. We give our deepest gratitude and appreciation to you (Glen) for investing in us."

Dr. Rick Hicks, President, Operation Mobilization, USA
Leadership Is—How to Build Your Legacy
"We have a choice in how we lead. Glen Aubrey, in his book *Leadership Is*—, lays out a road map to navigate these choices. As we follow his advice and become more intentional in our dealings with others, we are shown how to 'Lead well, and build people for life.'"

"It is a privilege for me to serve as a reference for Creative Team Resources Group... Glen has incredibly strong commitment to building teams... Many in the marketplace are aware of the need for effectiveness of team-building principles. The issues of building trust, educating, giving people parameters, having accountability, and freeing them up in their areas of creativity provide a work environment that can be healthier, happier and more effective in the long run.

"One of the effective tools that I have seen Glen use is this team-building process which builds strong, healthy, work relationships. That is, it helps people understand how they relate one to another, what their roles are, and how they need each other to fulfill the overall task as a team. It is easy to talk about team-building and relationship-building in the workforce. But to actually accomplish these tasks through the consulting process is quite difficult. I have seen Glen come into a situation with a very results-oriented perspective and an analytical approach, and be able to take the theory and apply it practically and effectively.

"If your situation warrants giving attention to the issue of team-building, I would recommend Creative Team Resources Group to you without reservation…"

Jerald Coleman, IT Director, Health and Human Services Agency, County of San Diego
Core Teams Work

"Like many organizations with technology-oriented staff, we like to attack and solve problems. *Leadership Is—* showed us how to open lines of communication. *Industrial Strength Solutions* reminded us to 'close the loop' to ensure our tasks were complete. *Core Teams Work* provides us with the principles and practices to promote effective communication amongst ourselves and with our customers."

Rick Perrotta, CEO, Rubicon Technology Group
Industrial Strength Solutions

"Principles of leadership, team building, character and change are the vital determining factors in today's competitive business landscape, and the critical characteristics in today's flatter world. This is value-added differentiation for business products, solutions, and relationships. Mature and potential leaders will absorb and commit to practicing the principles and methodologies outlined here which are reinforced with excellent 'real world' examples."

David A. Fisher, Partner, K&L Gates LLP
Leadership Is—How to Build Your Legacy

"With great difficulty, many have analyzed and some have well defined at least the qualities of leadership. Glen Aubrey superbly takes his readers into the more challenging domain of how to accomplish it."

"When we first met and I first considered retaining CTRG nothing could have prepared me for what I would learn or the results that would be achieved to date. We would do it again not only with no hesitation, but happily..."

John D. Kirby, Colonel (Retired), Vietnam Combat Veteran
1st Cavalry Division (Airmobile); Subsequently Attorney-at-Law, Litigation
Lessons of War—Lincoln's Second Inaugural Address, Leadership at Gettysburg

"Leadership—real, enduring leadership—is shown in *Lessons of War—Lincoln's Second Inaugural Address, Leadership at Gettysburg* to be that which is firmly grounded in and based upon reality and truth, coupled with genuine caring for those being led. This, in turn, leads to the best preparation for and conduct of the conflict. Glen Aubrey carries forward these critical leadership principals, and shows how to succeed in the next and final phase of every conflict—the ending of the conflict, with an accompanying establishment of genuine peace, or as close to genuine peace as is humanly possible, and Godly allowed. A must read for anyone who wishes his or her own conflicts, personal or organizational, to end well."

Arthur "Bud" Tickel, Chief of Water Operations, City of Fresno
DPU—Water Division

"I am proud to work for an organization that recognizes the importance of the leadership training you provide. Everyone has a different understanding of what they believe their leadership role should be and how it should affect those around them. Core Team Training provides a cohesive, comprehensive view of leadership, resulting in functional teams, operating under the same basic principles and practices."

Alisa Edwards, Realtor, Urban Homes Real Estate, San Diego

"I am a Realtor. I work for myself, considered an independent contractor in the State of California. It was interesting to me once we got into the team training, that I am part of several teams in my work environment. I do have a core team of people that I work with towards a common goal in each transaction. The tricks and tools I learned have helped to solidify the foundation of each team I work with and the way we communicate, as well as why we do what we do. I would recommend your class series to anyone looking to polish team communication and goal clarification. Thank you so much for all the coaching, it has provided a wonderful foundation for my everyday life, both work and home. You and your team are doing great things!"

Thomas R. Clark, RPh, MHS, Director of Policy and Advocacy
American Society of Consultant Pharmacists

"Your consulting services, along with Core Team training and Leadership Investment training, have been extremely useful to us... Your expertise, and especially your passion and commitment, have set an example for our staff and shown us how to put into practice the principles that you have been teaching. The training materials you supplied have provided a continuing reminder of those principles and have been an important part of the package of services for our company. The net impact of your services has been to improve working relationships and to provide key leaders with the knowledge and skills to maintain this improvement in the future... I would certainly encourage any business to take advantage of the services provided by your company."

Barry E. Willey, Colonel (Retired), U.S. Army
Author, *Out of the Valley* (Officers' Christian Fellowship, 2007)
Lessons of War—Lincoln's Second Inaugural Address, Leadership at Gettysburg

"Many Americans have never encountered Lincoln's Second Inaugural Address, nor fully appreciate the strategic importance of the Battle of Gettysburg in our nation's history. Glen Aubrey's *Lessons of War—Lincoln's Second Inaugural Address, Leadership at Gettysburg* brings both of these historically significant events together in a poignant way. He helps us see clearly that seeking peaceful resolution is the ultimate aim of those forced to participate in war and that good leaders "choose the best ways to conduct and conclude it." Aubrey's insights are captivating and compelling. Examples of sound leadership lessons and principles abound in every chapter. Former, current and aspiring leaders would be wise to learn them, savor them...and apply them as they lead. This is a future classic."

Stephen M. Annis, Sergeant (Retired), United States Air Force
Vietnam War Veteran 1966 – 1970
Executive Vice President and Chief Financial Officer, Valley Republic Bank
Lessons of War—Lincoln's Second Inaugural Address, Leadership at Gettysburg

"As an avid student of the nation-changing event we know as the Battle of Gettysburg, Glen Aubrey has now completed his second study of the lessons to be learned from that conflict and, more importantly, the lessons to be learned from studying the genius that was and is Abraham Lincoln. In *Lessons of War— Lincoln's Second Inaugural Address, Leadership at Gettysburg*, Glen opens our eyes to the message of hope, commitment, and faith in God that Lincoln so skillfully wove into his Second Inaugural Address. You cannot read this book without gaining enormous insight into Abraham Lincoln—the man. Glen then takes that insight and develops a clear understanding of how those truths can be used to enrich our own lives and leadership styles today."

Lincoln's Leadership—

If You Want Success, Lead Like This

Glen Aubrey

www.LincolnsLeadership.com

Creative Team Publishing
San Diego
www.CreativeTeamPublishing.com

© 2012 by Glen Aubrey.

All rights reserved. No part of this book may be reproduced, stored in a retrieval system or transmitted in any form or by any means without the prior written permission of the publisher, except by a reviewer who may quote brief passages in a review to be distributed through electronic media, or printed in a newspaper, magazine or journal.

Permissions and Credits:

Excerpts from *Lincoln, Leadership and Gettysburg—Defining Moments of Greatness* © 2009 by Glen Aubrey are used by permission of Glen Aubrey and Creative Team Publishing.

Excerpts from *Lessons of War—Lincoln's Second Inaugural Address, Leadership at Gettysburg* © 2011 by Glen Aubrey are used by permission of Glen Aubrey and Creative Team Publishing.

Text of First Inaugural Address and text of Second Inaugural Address by Abraham Lincoln, quotes and proclamations, are in the public domain.

Original source material for familiar Lincoln references including stories and anecdotes is in the public domain.

Quotes from *Essays: First Series* (1841) by Ralph Waldo Emerson are used by permission of http://www.emersoncentral.com as quoted in *Leadership Is—How to Build Your Legacy,* Copyright 2004 and 2012 by Glen Aubrey, and are used by permission of Glen Aubrey and Creative Team Publishing.

Additional references quoted from *Leadership Is—How to Build Your Legacy,* Copyright 2004 and 2012 by Glen Aubrey, are used by permission of Glen Aubrey and Creative Team Publishing.

Scripture taken from the *Holy Bible, New International Version.* (NIV) Copyright 1973, 1978, 1984 International Bible Society. Used by permission of Zondervan Bible Publishers. All rights reserved.

<u>Story Disclaimer</u>: Throughout *Lincoln's Leadership—If You Want Success, Lead Like This* stories are presented to illustrate salient points. All of the stories are true. In every case people's names and work situations or environments in which the stories occurred have been changed. Any resemblance to any known person, circumstance, situation, company, or environment is purely coincidental.

ISBN: 978-0-9855979-7-9
PUBLISHED BY CREATIVE TEAM PUBLISHING
www.CreativeTeamPublishing.com
San Diego
Printed in the United States of America

Lincoln's Leadership

If You Want Success, Lead Like This

Glen Aubrey

www.LincolnsLeadership.com

Table of Contents

Initial Thoughts
    Lincoln, the Effective Leader   23
        Lincoln letter to Horace Greeley,
            August 22, 1862   25
        A Proclamation by the President of the
            United States of America,
            September 24, 1862   28
        Newspaper article from the *Herald*,
            Richmond, Virginia, April 9, 1865
            "Visitors To Richmond"   32

Lesson 1
    Leadership's Effects   41
        A Definition of Leadership   42
        Action Always Births Reaction, Cause Always
            Produces Effect   44

Lesson 2
    Know Where You Are and Where You
    Are Going   47
        ROSA—Relationship and Operational
            Structure Analysis   49
        Excerpt from the "House Divided" Speech,
            Abraham Lincoln, June 16, 1858,
            Springfield, Illinois   50

Lesson 3
- Win and End Conflict Well — 53
  - Wars Are Part of the Human Experience — 54
  - We Know We Must Enter Them — 55
  - We Know How to Win Them — 57
  - Let Us Learn How to End Them Well — 58

Lesson 4
- Leadership Explains Cause and Effect — 63
  - Incidents and Issues — 65
  - Incidents and Issues Defined — 65

Lesson 5
- The Responsibility to Preserve and Defend Great Causes — 71
  - Excerpt from the First Inaugural Address, Abraham Lincoln, March 4, 1861, Washington, D.C. — 75
  - Excerpt from the Emancipation Proclamation, Abraham Lincoln, January 1, 1863, Washington, D.C. — 77

Lesson 6
- Words and Deeds Must Prove Each Other — 81
  - Declaration — 82
  - Clarity and Closure — 83
  - Excerpt from the Gettysburg Address, Abraham Lincoln, November 19, 1863, Gettysburg, Pennsylvania — 85

Lesson 7
    Enduring Leadership Principles Live for
    All Time   91

Lesson 8
    Learning Becomes Living When Behaviors
    Change   101
        The 13th Amendment to the Constitution of
            the United States   103
        Changing Behavior   105

Lesson 9
    Frameworks, Followers, and Fulfillment   107
        A Framework of Success: Teaching, Modeling,
            Encouragement, and Support   108
        Frameworks of Lasting Principles and
            Commitments   109

Lesson 10
    Truth Wins Because It Must   115
        Great Leadership Regenerates Itself   116
        Excerpt from the Declaration of
            Independence, July 4, 1776   123
        Excerpt from the "House Divided" Speech,
            Abraham Lincoln, June 16, 1858,
            Springfield, Illinois   124

Lesson 11
- Recognizing Conflict — 127
  - People Are More Important Than Production — 128
  - Relationship and Function — 129

Lesson 12
- Dealing with Conflict Is Not Optional — 133
  - Prepare for Conflict Because Conflict Is Unavoidable — 134
  - Farewell Speech, Abraham Lincoln, February 11, 1861, Springfield, Illinois — 140

Lesson 13
- How Strong Is Your Belief in Positive Results? — 145
  - Commitment to Success Is Shown in Action — 147
  - Sustainable Change — 148

Lesson 14
- What Is Cherished Today — 155
  - Sacrifice — 156
  - Be Thankful — 158
  - Excerpt from the Gettysburg Address, Abraham Lincoln, November 19, 1863, Gettysburg, Pennsylvania — 160

Lesson 15
- Legacies Last Beyond What Is Expedient — 163
  - Opinions Change, Principles Do Not — 165
  - Freedom — 166
  - Expedient vs. Excellent Leadership — 167

Lesson 16
    Leaders Learn and Get Involved   169
        Leaders Learn from History   170
        Belief and Action   173
        Taking Initiative   174

Lesson 17
    Responsibilities Accompany Remembrance and Retelling   177
        Teaching History   178
        Telling Stories   179

Lesson 18
    Leaders Recognize Their Limits   183
        Introduction to Lincoln's response on the Repeal of the Missouri Compromise   188
        Introduction to Lincoln's Peoria Speech on the Repeal of the Missouri Compromise   189

Lesson 19
    A Repeating Cycle of Cause and Effect   191
        The Law of Sowing and Reaping and the Law of Compensation   191
        Communication, Core principles, and Concrete Action   195

Lesson 20
- Consequences, Good or Bad 201
  - A Value System and the Effectiveness Proofs 203
  - Nine Proofs of a Value System's Validity and Endurance 207

Speech on the Repeal of the Missouri Compromise
Abraham Lincoln, October 16, 1854,
Peoria, Illinois 219

Address Delivered at the Dedication of the
Cemetery at Gettysburg, Abraham Lincoln,
November 19, 1863,
Gettysburg, Pennsylvania 293

Second Inaugural Address, Abraham Lincoln,
March 4, 1865. Washington, D.C. 295

Final Thoughts 299

Acknowledgements 303

Products and Services 311

Initial Thoughts
Lincoln, the Effective Leader

Few leaders have shaped the course of history as significantly as Abraham Lincoln. Calling the United States of America "the last best hope of earth" in correspondence with Congress in 1862, Lincoln not only bore the brunt of a Civil War that nearly destroyed that hope permanently, he rescued a nation in the process and that hope became reality. Interestingly, from the inception of his presidency to its close he never knew peace, yet he fashioned foundations for peace that have kept the country together and stronger ever since.

The results of Lincoln's leadership throughout the devastating conflicts of the Civil War were the reuniting of the Union and the freeing of the slaves. These two goals, the first as part of his official duty and the second his "oft-expressed personal wish" were outlined in correspondence with Horace Greely, Editor of the *New York Tribune* in August, 1862.

Understand that these two goals were both accomplished after Lincoln's death which occurred on April 14, 1865. The official "last land battle" of the war occurred two days after the president's assassination, and the official and permanent end of slavery came about with the ratification of the 13th Amendment on December 6, 1865.

From *Lincoln, Leadership and Gettysburg*, pages 63-65: "One of the most powerful letters ever given in defense of responsible action was Abraham Lincoln's reply to Horace Greeley. On August 19, 1862 Mr. Greeley, editor of the *New York Tribune*, published an open letter to the president in the form of an editorial entitled *The Prayer of Twenty Millions*. In this letter Greeley intimated that Lincoln's administration was floundering, purposeless, on the war.

"Lincoln responded to Greeley on August 22, 1862, as follows:

Executive Mansion,
Washington, August 22, 1862.

Hon. Horace Greeley:
Dear Sir.

I have just read yours of the 19th. addressed to myself through the New-York Tribune. As to the policy I "seem to be pursuing" as you say, I have not meant to leave any one in doubt.

I would save the Union. I would save it the shortest way under the Constitution. The sooner the national authority can be restored; the nearer the Union will be "the Union as it was." If there be those who would not save the Union, unless they could at the same time save slavery, I do not agree with them. If there be those who would not save the Union unless they could at the same time destroy slavery, I do not agree with them. My paramount object in this struggle is to save the Union, and is not either to save or to destroy slavery. If I could save the Union without freeing any slave I would do it, and if I could save it by freeing all the slaves I would do it; and if I could save it by freeing some and leaving others alone I would also do that. What I do about slavery, and the colored race, I do because I believe it helps to save the Union; and what I forbear, I forbear because I do not believe it would help to save the Union. I shall do less whenever I shall believe what I am doing hurts the cause, and I shall do more whenever I shall believe doing more will help the cause. I shall try to correct errors when shown to be errors; and I shall adopt new views so fast as they shall appear to be true views.

I have here stated my purpose according to my view of official duty; and I intend no modification of my oft-expressed personal wish that all men everywhere could be free.

Yours,

A. Lincoln."

Some might argue, even convincingly, that Lincoln was politically motivated throughout his presidency while he desperately sought to save the country. He took extreme measures like suspending the *writ of habeas corpus* in 1861 for Maryland and some parts of the Midwestern states, eventually doing so for the entire nation in 1862.

Further, some believe that his election and subsequent actions as president in the early days of his first term actually brought about the onset of the Civil War or, at a minimum, caused the internal disruption that led to the South firing on Fort Sumter on April 12, 1861.

Finger pointing continues to this day about the effects of Lincoln's choices and activities. Opinions, regardless if pro-Lincoln or anti-Lincoln, should be considered on the basis of the historical record.

For example, there is no doubt that Lincoln defied the Supreme Court and issued this proclamation on Sept. 24, 1862:

Glen Aubrey

BY THE PRESIDENT OF THE UNITED STATES OF AMERICA:

A PROCLAMATION

Whereas, it has become necessary to call into service not only volunteers but also portions of the militia of the States by draft in order to suppress the insurrection existing in the United States, and disloyal persons are not adequately restrained by the ordinary processes of law from hindering this measure and from giving aid and comfort in various ways to the insurrection;

Now, therefore, be it ordered, first, that during the existing insurrection and as a necessary measure for suppressing the same, all Rebels and Insurgents, their aiders and abettors within the United States, and all persons discouraging volunteer enlistments, resisting militia drafts, or guilty of any disloyal practice, affording aid and comfort to Rebels against the authority of United States, shall be subject to martial law and liable to trial and punishment by Courts Martial or Military Commission:

Second. That the Writ of Habeas Corpus is suspended in respect to all persons arrested, or who are now, or hereafter during the rebellion shall be, imprisoned in any fort, camp, arsenal, military prison, or other place of confinement by any military authority of by the sentence of any Court Martial or Military Commission.

In witness whereof, I have hereunto set my hand, and caused the seal of the United States to be affixed.

Done at the City of Washington this twenty fourth day of September, in the year of our Lord one thousand eight hundred and sixty-two, and of the Independence of the United States the 87th.

ABRAHAM LINCOLN
By the President:
WILLIAM H. SEWARD, Secretary of State.

The extreme conflict tore at the very fabric of the nation and sought to unravel it forever. These circumstances called for extraordinary and unprecedented measures the nation's leader chose to take. In his role as president he was convinced he had no other option than to do what he did. Whether or not Lincoln was justified in his actions, he took them, and the results speak for themselves.

Lincoln's Leadership—If You Want Success, Lead Like This does not seek to address or answer the arguments about whether or not the president was right or wrong in his actions. Those arguments are not a part of course of this study. Rather, this book addresses living leadership principles and practices of a master leader, a gifted and highly intelligent individual who won the war and accomplished his stated goals though his victories required extreme sacrifice and ultimately cost him his life.

The leadership Lincoln exercised brought about restoration for a shattered and divided Union. The wages of this accomplishment were horrendous, interweaving supreme struggles, mighty travail, and severely cruel and long-lingering aftermaths of a civil war. Was reuniting the Union worth it?

Thoughtful leaders have no choice but to weigh the costs of decision making when the costs are known, and make the choices that, more often than not, outlast the very causes their choices address. Even when costs are unknown, the leader still has to decide, and many must endure the consequences of those decisions, right or wrong.

Lincoln's Leadership—If You Want Success, Lead Like This highlights remarkable and enduring leadership principles and practices that Lincoln embraced. It shows how these leadership truths can and should be exercised in contemporary business and personal interactions with others. When they are framed within the context of positive desires for the betterment of mankind, their results can be nothing short of breathtaking, meritorious, positive, uplifting, encouraging, hope-inspiring, and long lasting.

This book asks the leader who wants to embrace Lincoln's leadership truths to count the costs as well as the rewards of their application. The book requests that leaders define their motives as well as their methods. Both must be weighed on the scales of great leadership. It's never one to the exclusion of the other. It's never all motive, or all method. For effective leadership to be present, a balance is required.

It is curious on one level and sad on another that Lincoln did not live to see the actual conclusion of the war he so desperately declared he wanted to avoid. He certainly witnessed the sights and sounds of Richmond's downfall. In fact, with his son Tad he visited Richmond on April 4 and 5, 1865 after the Confederate government had evacuated the city on April 3.

Lincoln knew that when Lee surrendered this act would eventually bring about the complete cessation of the war. From the time he visited Richmond, he didn't have to wait long until the capitulation at Appomattox occurred. Robert E. Lee surrendered to Ulysses S. Grant on April 9, 1865.

Events moved rapidly that week. Some of the changes that occurred in Richmond over the next few days were chronicled in the New York *Herald* on April 12, 1865:

> RICHMOND.
> Mr. William H. Merriam's Despatches [*sic*].
> RICHMOND, April 9, 1865.
> VISITORS TO RICHMOND.
>
> Richmond is still enveloped in excitement, and I cannot perceive as yet any abatement. It leaves

the truth somewhat in the rear to say that almost everybody eminent has visited and is now viewing the precincts of this captured city. The provost marshals of the North must grow lean with labor in supplying passes to the regiments, brigades, divisions, corps and columns of people who are knocking at these gates for admission. The President of the United States came and saw, and, it may be added, conquered; Senators and legislators of less degree followed in rapid succession; and in all the throng yesterday I noticed the Vice President, accompanied by Senator Sumner, riding along Clay street in an ambulance; but I shall not stop to notice or name the long array of eminent men and lovely women who have flocked to this city since Monday last.

Lincoln was assassinated on Friday, April 14, 1865 at Ford's Theater in Washington, D.C. The final battle of the Civil War occurred in Columbus, Alabama on April 16, 1865. According to the information on the plaque commemorating the event at the location: "LAST LAND BATTLE IN WAR OF 1861- 65: The last important land battle of the War Between the States was fought here April 16, 1865, resulting in the capture of Columbus by Federal forces. The engagement began directly west of Columbus in Alabama and ended on the Georgia side of the Chattahoochee. The defending line of the entrenchments (in Alabama) was more than a mile in length. Artillery mounted on high hills was used in the action. Both cavalry and infantry engaged in the battle."

While Lincoln missed the actual close of the Civil War, his leadership had already laid the foundation for a peace that would sustain the reunified country throughout its next phases of history, across many decades of internal strife and hard-won adjustment. Peace was not easy to achieve or enforce—most peace agreements are not. Yet, where positive outcomes are strongly desired, leaders with vision, acting on principle, anticipate the future as they conclude that peace is more desirable than continuous conflict. These leaders seek solutions that will bring about improved and most desirable results though the costs are very high indeed.

The leadership truths presented in *Lincoln's Leadership—If You Want Success, Lead Like This* are drawn from the leadership principles revealed in three of Lincoln's greatest speeches: his Gettysburg Address, his Second Inaugural Address, and a not as well known but profound address that predated both, his Speech on the Repeal of the Missouri Compromise delivered on October 16, 1854 at Peoria, Illinois.

Selected truths presented in two prior books by this author, *Lincoln, Leadership and Gettysburg* (2009) and *Lessons of War— Lincoln's Second Inaugural Address, Leadership at Gettysburg* (2011) are showcased, but within the perspective of practical application in arenas of human relationships, business environments, and workplace teams. The illustrations within the Peoria speech are nothing short of remarkable as they graphically display higher causes and the developing leadership that stands for the right, no matter what the future holds.

If those in charge want to improve their leadership skills they can seldom discover a greater example after which to model their behaviors than the one of Abraham Lincoln. His leadership touched personal and working relationships on broad fronts. It brought opposing parties together, and in the case of the 13th Amendment, firmly and forever established a law built on the timeless principle of human freedom and equality.

Great leadership lessons like those of Lincoln endure because they are founded on solid and enduring truth. It is up to current leaders to learn and embrace these bedrock truths and utilize them fully in *their* real life situations.

History is replete with lessons that contemporary society must observe, learn, and incorporate. If one generation doesn't learn history's repeatable proofs, history with its negative consequences will be repeated—at least until the lessons are learned by a single generation.

Some of these lessons we must never forget. They are surrounded by names contemporary society vividly recalls. To name a few: Pearl Harbor, the Holocaust of Nazi Germany in WWII, and more recently, 911 (September 11, 2001). Enduring lessons have emerged from these tragedies that we must remember with cause to be sure we **never** permit events like these to happen again.

Reach back even farther and learn the lessons that motivated Lincoln. The environments in which his leadership was exercised not only framed his leadership; his leadership formed those environments. This is how it should be.

Learn Lincoln's leadership and why it worked. To do so, learn the environments and the effects. Then apply the lessons of his Civil War leadership to events and circumstances of today.

That is exactly what we will do in this book. This exercise will help us know better not only what we face when leadership challenges present themselves, it will also help us understand how we can and should shape and even remake our environments to align with eternal truths that produce better and positive uplifting results whenever they are followed.

People must be led. Leadership abhors a vacuum; this truth is well known. The question is never if leadership will respond to a need. The question always is, "What kinds of leadership will the leader enact to achieve the most desirable results?"

The kinds of leadership models that are chosen and applied by the one in charge of any group will demonstrate stark differences between positive, enduring methods and negative, disreputable outcomes. The leader bears tremendous responsibility to choose the leadership models and methods that have been proven through time to enhance human relationships and experiences, those that ultimately improve the opportunities and options of those who follow.

A country, state, county, city, corporate team, or business of any size will be positively affected by the lessons presented in *Lincoln's Leadership—If You Want Success, Lead Like This*. Why? When *enduring* leadership truths are practiced by leaders who truly care about their people as well as what they can produce, great results will happen though processes may be long and the journey unpleasant at times. Truth wins in the end because it must.

The worth of every person commands that those who lead strive to do so to the best of their ability so that all are benefitted, no matter the odds arrayed against them. Knowing that sacrifice very likely is or will become a part of the price the effective leader will have to pay, he or she perseveres anyway.

Not all leadership models work well, nor should they. Not all leaders are effective, nor should they be. Not all people who fill the position of leader embrace what great leadership really is. In fact, leaders who lead like Lincoln are few because the costs are deemed by many to be too high, and shallow leadership rejects paying them.

Leadership is less about title, position, stature, or inherent gifting and far more about one individual's desire to make great choices about the success of another. Herein is right leadership formed and practiced. Within this leadership paradigm it's about standing on right principle and sacrificing for it if sacrifice is required.

The effective leader may have to give more than he or she receives. This is a hard truth for some to embrace, but it's true nonetheless. The strong and effective leader quickly learns that one of the most important gifts he or she can give to those who follow is the instruction and modeling that helps prepare the follower to accomplish more than the leader ever could. How many leaders do you know who have done this? Those who do produce enduring results for succeeding generations much like Lincoln did. Those leaders produce positive legacy.

If you are one of those who want to join the ranks of steadfast and superior leaders, read on. Learn and apply the principles in these pages. Perhaps a family will be helped, a career rescued or begun, a primary motivation renewed, or methods of accomplishing worthy goals reinvigorated. It is up to great leaders to ever remain students and practitioners of right leadership principles and practices, to learn the lessons well, weigh the costs, act upon what they know is right, and create improving and enduring environments for all.

A leader will touch many in his or her impact, influence, and investment efforts.* The results of these efforts stand the greatest chance of success because the heart of the leader reflects the characteristics of right and enduring principle. His or her actions will corroborate the core of his or her character. Followers will be drawn to this person because that's how leadership works. Results follow this leader's contributions, whether or not he or she witnesses them first hand. (*See *Leadership Is—How to Build Your Legacy* Revised Version, by Glen Aubrey, © 2012, www.LeadershipIs.com for a full description of impact, influence, and investment leadership.)

Leadership matters. *Lincoln's Leadership—If You Want Success, Lead Like This* provides enduring models of tried and tested leadership principles. Great leaders will learn and emulate them.

We will explore how one takes the matters of leadership and makes them active in any situation where the true essence of leading well and seeing positive results are the objects of the efforts expended. If you are ready, let's begin.

Lesson 1
Leadership's Effects

"Effects endure beyond the events that give them life. Learn their truths. History's lessons shape the minds and means of generations." (*Lincoln, Leadership and Gettysburg*, page 5)

A leader must learn history if he or she is going to lead with effectiveness in any current environment. Use of the term *effectiveness* is intentional. Leadership isn't leadership unless it produces positive effects.

It's all about human interaction and what comes from it. Little is new and much is predictable especially when it comes to how human beings relate to each other. The verse rings true: "What has been will be again, what has been done will be done again; there is nothing new under the sun." (Ecclesiastes 1:9 NIV)

Lincoln knew this truth. He was a master of the study of how people interact. That trait was one reason his communication was so effective in speeches before and during his presidency.

A Definition of Leadership

Early in the course of writing the first version *Leadership Is—How to Build Your Legacy* I framed a definition of leadership. It is this: "… leadership is a state of interaction with others that can and must be cultivated to create duplicative results for positive and regenerating impact." Further, "Followers look to leaders to provide examples of how to follow as well as lead. That truth simply adds more importance to leading and following well where following and leading are patterned according to a regenerating model where character and consistency are the motivators." (See *Leadership Is—How to Build Your Legacy* Revised Version, page 17.)

Leadership at its core is solely a *state of interaction*. Without more than one person present there is no leadership because there is no one to lead, or follow. With more than one person present a state of interaction exists. The person who takes the initiative becomes the point person of proof and he or she determines the quality of both the leadership opportunity and its action.

If that state of interaction is cultivated with the right motives in mind—seeds planted in good soil and nourished, with their fruit harvested in the expectation that something greater than what had existed was being produced—the results should be seen in duplicative, positive, and regenerating impact, exponential in effect.

Leadership is never done in a vacuum. It is always present and accounted for in the moment when it occurs. Its outcomes will be seen over time in the lives of the people it touches.

Take the impact portion away from leadership and we are left with merely a collection of ideas resembling a sort of pabulum. It's tolerable but it doesn't nourish long-term.

When leadership is conducted correctly coming from the right motives it will produce results, period. These fruits will become part of the history of the interaction between leader and follower and that history will endure as long as the memory and impact of the moment endure.

What is perhaps not appreciated as much as it should is this truth: history places its stamp of approval or disapproval on the quality of any interaction where leadership is exercised strictly on the basis of the *results* the interaction produces. These results can be good or bad, uplifting or degrading, truthful or dishonest, destined to produce positive outcomes, or designed to bring forth disreputable and rotten fruit which represent the negative effects current and future generations will seek to discard.

Action Always Births Reaction, Cause Always Produces Effect

A leader is anyone who takes the initiative. He or she will reap the harvest of the quality of their interaction with any follower, and the follower will share in these results as well. The effects of an interaction, regardless of size, do not endure for only a moment without residual impacts. Action always births reaction, cause always produces effect.

Great leaders, therefore, strive for beneficial outcomes with a follower in every interaction regardless of size because they are convinced that the results will not be confined to just a single moment. In Lincoln's case, he was well aware that virtually everything he said would carry great weight, and this was one reason why he never wanted to speak in public without being fully prepared.

Results of a leader's interaction with a follower become part of history, their history, and perhaps the history of others who are touched. Lessons learned will always shape the minds and means of generations present and those to come.

The effects of Lincoln's leadership during the era of the Civil War produced impacts far beyond what Mr. Lincoln could likely have ever imagined. He literally shaped the minds and the means of a divided nation, restoring its unity despite the great costs of doing so.

The *mind* of a generation is composed of what it believes—the principles it is convinced are true. The *means* of a generation are the tasks a group of individuals strives to accomplish because of what they believe. These two—belief and practice, mind and means—are inseparable.

How important is leadership within a state of an interaction between two people or more? It is vital. Understand that leadership is never isolated in its action or its effects. It is always impactful to some degree.

Results endure beyond its birth and can change the course of life for many. Therefore, if you are the leader, grow wise in your understanding and appreciation of the responsibility and execution you bear as you lead. You may never become as well known as Lincoln, but the application of leadership truths in your methods may well endure beyond you and become part of your legacy.

Lesson 2
Know Where You Are and Where You Are Going

"I need help." This pleading admission came at the conclusion of a lengthy but important conversation with a potential client of Creative Team Resources Group (CTRG, www.ctrg.com). Our meeting had been requested by him, and as part of our processes of prequalification I agreed to come over in person and discuss his company's situation.

What he described was not good. Dysfunction born of distrust and disengagement permeated the working atmosphere of his firm. These negative conditions were affecting production and the bottom line of this company of 175 employees. Customer service reports showed a distinct and growing lack of interest in caring about customer satisfaction. The staff was being treated poorly by middle managers who seemed highly insecure in their own positions, and blame for the gross inequities was everywhere.

The CEO who had asked for our meeting appeared to be threatened as his board of directors and major stakeholders were growing restless and wanted change, and they wanted it *now*. As sharp as he was (and he was brilliant), his tasks seemed overwhelming, though he knew upon being hired six months prior that one of his major roles was to right the wrongs and get the company back on track no matter what it cost or who he had to replace.

He knew his responsibility and accepted it, but his basic question was, "Where do I even start?" That was the point where CTRG had been invited in.

ROSA—Relationship and Operational Structure Analysis

One of the products our firm uses to ascertain condition and need and opportunity for success is called ROSA (ROSA © 2012 Creative Team Resources Group). It stands for Relationship and Operational Structure Analysis. It is a highly effective tool that delves beneath the surface of complaining, bitterness, and finger-pointing, to reach a point of discovery of levels of ownership of solution provision. ROSA is a determiner of future engagement; if on the basis of what we discover we deem it true that we really can't help an organization improve, we simply will state this. In our entire history we have had to state this only twice to date, once in a non-profit organization, and again in a for-profit company whose name is well known.

The ROSA process, including its Acquaintance Seminar, confidential interviews, analysis, and reports reveals conditions of right action, problems and wrong action, and then demonstrates degrees of ownership that may exist on the part of the people who have articulated the problems. We have found that to the degree a person bringing a problem to the forefront wants to be involved in a solution to the problem, the chances for positive changes increase dramatically. The reverse is also true: to the degree that the person who describes the problem does not want to be a part of the solution the chances for success decrease remarkably.

A leader has to determine degrees of ownership of solutions from those he or she leads. Without asking questions and seeking to build opportunities of positive engagement from the followers, the leader or leadership team may likely flounder as they confront incidents and issues that consume their time and drain their energy and pocketbook.

Excerpt from the "House Divided" Speech, Abraham Lincoln, June 16, 1858, Springfield, Illinois

Such was the situation in 1858 as Lincoln delivered his "A House Divided" speech before the Republican State Convention of Illinois at Springfield on June 16. The event occurred two years before the presidential election of 1860, and the points of disconnect and dysfunction Lincoln addressed were vast. Lincoln rightly concluded that he needed to take his listeners back to the beginning of the creation of the country, to help frame an understanding of what had been and where they were then, to be able to more correctly chart a course for the future.

In his singular style, Lincoln opened his speech with the following words: *"If we could first know where we are, and whither we are tending, we could better judge what to do, and how to do it."* In other words, success was conditional on knowing a current condition and how it came about. Only then could the goals for success be defined. The basis of the knowledge of the origin of current condition would help Lincoln's listeners form correct judgments about how to proceed, to right the wrongs the country was currently facing.

Here's the counsel: if a dysfunction seems too great or the problems insurmountable and you as the leader feel like you don't know where to start to correct the situation, begin with discovery. Find out where you are and how you got there. Relate the current situation to the goals of success that likely were part of the framework of your positional placement in the first place, as well as the company's Values, Vision, Mission, and Message, the Code of Achievement as described in the Revised Version of *Leadership Is—How to Build Your Legacy*, Chapter 5. Upon that knowledge you and your team will better be able to determine what to do and how to do it.

Without knowledge, confusion reigns. Confusion is born of lack of correct information and often resides in shallow opinions, feelings, and whims. With accurate knowledge, however, comes increased wisdom. Rallying your team around the truth of history and impartial analysis of the facts, can help chart a course for correction and success of a current situation.

Lesson 3
Win and End Conflict Well

Conflict will always be a part of the workplace experience. Wherever more than one person is present in any environment conflict is possible, of course, but conflict in the workplace is a condition that bears addressing because it is so prevalent. Left unchecked, or conducted outside of appropriate boundaries, workplace conflict can do great damage. Conducted appropriately, however, it can actually foster benefits. So because it's present, great leaders deal with it.

In *Lessons of War—Lincoln's Second Inaugural Address, Leadership at Gettysburg* a four-sentence introduction provided a frame of reference for the entire book: "Wars are part of the human experience. We know we must enter them. We know how to win them. Let us learn how to end them well."

Whether wars occur within a family, a company, a government, or between nations, the principles of war are the same. A wise leader recognizes these truths and addresses them.

Wars Are Part of the Human Experience

First: "Wars are part of the human experience." The difference between a conflict and a war may be the degree of unrest and rebellion as well as the strengths of commitment to certain beliefs that propel proponents to reject the beliefs of another. No matter the how big the differences, the simple truth is that conflict or war, or both, exist in the human experience, regardless of degree or location.

It is completely fruitless for any leader to think that if he or she is effective conflict won't occur. That is delusion. In fact, not all conflict is bad and it is sometimes encouraged, especially where creative and diverse thinking emerges from deliberate and respectful discourse. Varied opinions of many can frame a context for coming up with great ideas. Conflict, where mutual respect is present, can be one of the greatest contributors to solution thinking and acting.

Negative conflict, however, crosses the line and violates dignity. It showcases disrespect. It's where compromise is not possible or perhaps desired, and personal disconnect and team disruption become the children of opposing views. It's where people entrenched in their own beliefs and actions refuse even to listen to other points of view, and in the process undermine creative discussion and silence respectful interchange.

No matter if positive or negative, conflicts and wars are a part of the human experience, so don't try to avoid them. Rather, channel them when they come. Creatively deal with negative conflicts up front because you have to. By the same token, stimulate the kind of "positive" conflict you want because you desire input from opposing ideologies, but not to the point of violating mutual respect.

We Know We Must Enter Them

And this is the second principle: "We know we must enter them." Entering a conflict is a part of recognizing the problem and providing a solution to it. When a leader is leading well, this principle and practice is expected for the leader and his or her followers.

People who claim to be leaders, no matter their title or tenure, who allow conflicts to grow beyond the limit of creative stimulation, are not good leaders. In fact, they are failing in their duties to lead at all. *How* a leader chooses to enter any conflict is a consideration of entering at all.

President Lincoln sought to provision Fort Sumter in 1861. The fort was a Union outpost in the Charleston Harbor, South Carolina. He did so because it was his duty to see that the forts of the United States possessed the supplies they needed to fulfill their duties. When he chose to take care of the needs of this outpost, the South opened fire and the Civil War began.

There is a profound leadership truth here and it is this: a leader must do what is right according to the dictates of his or her position and the right standing of a cause to which he or she is committed, even if it means creating or fostering an unsettling environment where the opposing party acts to wage war and begins its attacks.

We Know How to Win Them

This leads us to the third principle: "We know how to win them." Most of the time, this is true. "Winning" may be defined in several ways. To some, winning is the complete conquering and subjugation of any perceived or real enemy. To others, winning may be the exercise of applying wisdom to a broad range of circumstances, weighing the costs, and because of the information received and believed, being willing to settle for less than all-out victory if in fact the case merits measured action. In the teachings of many religions, winning is seen as "turning the other cheek" or "sacrifice" or "loving your enemy." Regardless of the meaning of a "win" a leader must *define* what the win is at the outset of a conflict and know *precisely* what is required to achieve it. Only then can the proper course be charted to accomplish the goal. Perhaps nothing is worse than a war without a definition of a win.

All forms of winning must be weighed. These forms are generally dictated by the nature of the cause and the conflict, as well as the strengths and capabilities of the parties engaged in it. Great leaders seek to learn how to win, but only after they clearly define what winning is. Without this knowledge, entering the fray may be completely useless and cost the lives and fortunes of many needlessly.

Let Us Learn How to End Them Well

Finally for this lesson: "Let us learn how to end them well." From *Lessons of War—Lincoln's Second Inaugural Address, Leadership at Gettysburg*, page 22: "Leaders, patriots, and peace lovers understand the value of ending conflicts well. These people of principle look to Lincoln's example. These individuals strive '...*to do all which may achieve and cherish a just, and a lasting peace, among ourselves, and with all nations.*'"

To achieve and cherish a just and a lasting peace within and without are the goals of a committed and principled leader. This leader understands that just because a conflict is concluded or won (no matter the definition of a win), the residual affects must also be charted from the outset of the engagement.

A leader must desire to know and put forth the due diligence to determine what the end will look like before an engagement is commenced. If distance and permanent dissolution between former combatants is the context of a just and lasting peace, this component must be determined. If restitution and reconciliation between former opposing parties is the goal, this element must be decided.   Choices as to conduct come from these considerations.

Herein abides one of the greatest opportunities for leaders who understand that they must set the pace: they must see the broader picture, not merely its segments. Superior leaders view and anticipate a situation's end from its beginning and identify to the best of their knowledge what the conflict's cessation should and therefore must produce according to the principles they espouse.

In Lincoln's case he wanted restitution, preferring to treat the Southern states with dignity as they reentered the Union. His closing lines of the Second Inaugural Address began with these words which set the tone for how he wanted to end conflict well: "With malice toward none; with charity for all; with firmness in the right, as God gives us to see the right, let us strive on to finish the work we are in; to bind up the nation's wounds; to care for him who shall have borne the battle, and for his widow, and his orphan…"

What was he saying? *All* the action that was to define "ending conflict well" would emerge from three core beliefs and desires:

1. The absence of malice
2. The presence of love
3. The commitment to truth-principles as revealed by God

These characteristics of reuniting the country would be revealed in the following actions:

1. Finish the work: win the war. End the conflict according to prescribed and agreed tenets of victory.
2. Begin the process of healing.
3. Show compassion and care to those who engaged in the conflict and to all who were touched by it.

Leaders do well to apply these maxims. Ask yourself, "What are the core beliefs and desires that I know will constitute ending conflict well in my situation?" Don't go to the next question until that one is answered and the answer is agreed upon by those who will be involved in how the end will be conducted.

Then ask yourself, "What are the actions that must emerge from these core beliefs and commitments?" The three actions Lincoln espoused are revealing:

1. Finish what you need to do because you are committed to a just course of action. Unfinished business and conditions of unresolved agendas do not create atmospheres of lasting restitution or finality.

2. The healing process can take a long time, but it can only begin once the conflict is over. When healing begins, understand that wounds may be fresh, sores may still be open, remedies will take time (usually more than is expected or desired), and that scars will likely remain. Define what "healing" is or should be on the basis of the agreement of former opposing parties. This action may be just as important as determining what a win is. In fact, providing concise definitions of healing and winning may be integral to achieving the success of both.

3. Above all, show compassion. Humility takes its place as the leader of resolution when ego is set aside and helping replaces hurting. In this chosen environment of love, giving back replaces taking, and working toward assisting those who need it replaces hatred and malice.

Lesson 4

Leadership Explains Cause and Effect

Some people may be content to live and work apart from any knowledge of cause and effect. For the vast majority, however, a desire to know and understand the *why* in relation to the *what*, is a priority.

Explaining cause and effect is an effective leader's responsibility. Even where all the facts cannot be known regarding a condition or potential action, leaders try to see the larger view and base decisions, choices, and results on accurate information. Then they communicate to their followers their reasons for actions.

From *Lincoln, Leadership and Gettysburg*, page 17: "Great leadership frames defining moments as it seeks to explain cause and effect." Indeed, the defining moments are most readily seen when the larger picture is viewed and addressed.

This, of course, is exactly what Lincoln did for his audience and the country in his Gettysburg Address. The president sought to position the Civil War in the context of the young nation's history, its war-infused present, and its hope-endowed future. When he did (in less than two minutes), he defined the moment, movement, and methods of achieving "a new birth of freedom." The speech is a classic presentation and a model of communication effectiveness from leader to followers.

When a leader wants to communicate clearly, the terms that will be used have to be defined. Effective communication is not only dependent on what the originator says; it is also dependent on what the listener hears. This is especially true when it comes to identifying events and causes, or incidents and issues.

Incidents and Issues

At CTRG we differentiate between two terms, *incidents* and *issues* when we speak of problem identification and resolution. The differences often compose defining moments of comprehension and problem solving for a team whose members "get it" and apply what they've learned.

Incidents and Issues Defined

Work with your teams to assure they understand these two terms and that they act upon that understanding when they experience the need to identify areas of concern and work toward resolutions to them.

- *Incidents* are occurrences either man-made or circumstantial. They are the events that touch people regardless of their source. Incidents are tangible actions, events in place and time. They are words and works. They are evidenced by any who experience them.
- *Issues* are the reasons behind the incidents, the causes of the action or event. Issues are generally intangible and are often classified as validations or violations of values. Values cannot be bought or sold, of course. When they

are present we know, and when they are absent, we know that, too. Positive values constitute traits of human character such as trust, confidence, assurance, hope, truth, consistency, obedience, relationships, accountability, and integrity.

We teach leaders to recognize incidents. They have to see them. We also show that leaders rarely try to solve an incident on its own merit apart from understanding its root causes.

Weak leaders dwell in incidents and spin their wheels dealing with them. Little or no progress results toward lasting solution provision.

Great leaders, however, look for the reasons behind an action or an event. They address the issues because they want lasting resolution. They know that the issues compose the *why* behind the *what*, and that the only way to produce more permanent positive effects is to deal with both in balance.

Ineffective leaders may not see value in moving beyond incidents to solutions. But if solutions to incidents are to be effective they will emerge from an understanding of issues. Fixes based on addressing incidents alone last but temporarily.

If policies and procedures are used to correct inappropriate actions or decidedly wrong behaviors and a law says that a policy must be followed to address them, obedience to that law may not be optional. But this method may ignore the far more important and lasting impacts of addressing deeper causes of actions.

Addressing the *why* as well as *what* can help leaders and followers determine and design better results as resolution or restitution is accomplished. This is simply going to the source of the problem to fix it and not dealing with symptoms alone.

There is no negative incident that arises between two people, where the action of one causes disruption or negative impact to the other, which is not driven by some form of relational dysfunction. In other words, incidents fashioned by humans are never separated from desire and motive. Determine the cause of a negative occurrence and a leader can address a negative incident with far more knowledge and command, basing corrective action on more informed understanding.

The list of person-to-person conflicts in the workplace is unending, as the list of laws to address them. There simply are not enough policies, procedures, and laws to address every single negative human behavior that comes along, although many human resource professionals believe they are tasked with creating policies, procedures, or laws for each one.

Clearly where law is present, adherence to it is vital. However, when it comes to matters of human behavior, at some point causes must be addressed if laws are to even make sense.

In fact, where law and cause are brought together, where right issues elicit appropriate definitions of right behaviors, law will be recognized as appropriate, right, and true. Plus, it has a greater chance of being willingly followed.

As the leader, you will recognize incidents in your workplace that require correction. Our counsel is to address the immediate situation but move as expeditiously as possible to discovery of the reasons why an incident occurred and deal with the issues, too.

Ask yourself: "What are the recent incidents in my workplace that should be solved at the point of their issues?" Come up with an example where a system of operation was broken because one person failed to accomplish a task upon which another task by the next person depended. What issue was violated? Was it trust, care, consideration, security, competence, obedience, or something else?

Begin to think like this when you address the incidents in your team or company. Solve incidents if you must at the point of occurrence with policy, procedure, and law. Addressing an incident in this way may be required initially.

Don't live there, however. Move to the issues.

Teach the people of your teams to see the issues, uphold right causes, and produce more positive and long lasting effects. If you're the leader, you set the pace of dealing with incidents and their issues in balance.

Lesson 5
The Responsibility to Preserve and Defend Great Causes

Two great causes defined Lincoln's role as President of the United States. As was stated in the Introduction, the first one he deemed his "official duty" and it was to save the Union. The second one was what he termed his "personal wish" that "all men everywhere could be free."

These two tenets formed his platform and framed his activity. While stating them was not complicated, achieving them certainly was.

Great leaders learn and then earn the responsibilities inherent in preserving and defending great causes. One cannot exist without the other and the sequence is important.

Learning must come first. What life truths, bold beliefs, and immovable principles define a great cause for you? Think back to how you learned the core principles that help to shape your sense of right and wrong, duty and responsibility, cause and effect. What were the sources of your learning?

At CTRG we are convinced that the essentials of your composite nature are made up of three elements: experience, education, and environment. When a person is very young, these elements are usually decided for him or her. As maturity occurs, the growing person chooses the experiences in which he or she will live and work, the education that must be acquired, and the environments that contribute to well being and meritorious contribution. These choices are much like Lincoln's two tenets: while easy to state, they are sometimes very hard to accomplish.

Sources of learning are parts of the courses of learning and the development of a worldview. Input, regardless of origin, contributes to the processes of making decisions about right and wrong. Decisions for action based on worldviews birth choices of deeds that define the greater causes they support. An effective leader will espouse and try to fulfill the choices he or she makes because of a firmly held belief that the decisions are right.

As maturity occurs, long-held principles will be challenged, and they should be. Those that withstand life's ongoing tests are usually those that have held up through extended periods of time in the trials of human experience. These should be weighed carefully as new ideas are received and evaluated.

Experience, education, and environment cooperate to generate belief structures and the actions that proceed from them. They also continue to validate the causes that merit activities designed to accomplish noteworthy goals.

Responsibility for action comes with knowledge of right and wrong and the choices that arise from that knowledge. A leader who learns and is convinced of the truthfulness of his or her belief system will prove how convinced he or she is by his or her corroborating actions. That leader earns the responsibility of upholding what he or she knows to be true, and often fulfills that responsibility at great sacrifice.

Beliefs that are strong enough produce actions that are bold enough to create experiences, educational opportunities, and improved environments that are big enough for the leader and others *if* the leader is convinced enough to turn thoughts into deeds and words into works. It is one thing to express an opinion; it is quite another to act upon a belief especially when that belief goes against the status quo or a long-held traditional form of operation.

Engaged leaders are faced with the challenge and opportunity to learn from the past and project to the future. They rest their core beliefs on immovable and proven principles, and then chart courses of action designed to achieve results that benefit all.

Right causes that have endured are those for which freedom-loving people will sacrifice themselves if they are convinced of their value. Preserving a great cause often means defending a mechanism designed to promote that cause in perpetuity. Providing an environment in which individual freedom is present and encouraged and personal development can occur certainly is one of those causes.

Excerpt from the First Inaugural Address, Abraham Lincoln, March 4, 1861, Washington, D.C.

Lincoln was firmly committed to preserving the Union because he was convinced that it was birthed by men who believed in the perpetuity of the country. He had argued forcefully in his First Inaugural Address: "The Union is much older than the Constitution. It was formed, in fact, by the Articles of Association in 1774. It was matured and continued by the Declaration of Independence in 1776. It was further matured, and the faith of all the then thirteen States expressly plighted and engaged that it should be perpetual, by the Articles of Confederation in 1778. And finally, in 1787, one of the declared objects for ordaining and establishing the Constitution was 'to form a more perfect Union.'

"But if destruction of the Union by one or by a part only of the States be lawfully possible, the Union is less perfect than before the Constitution, having lost the vital element of perpetuity.

"It follows from these views that no State upon its own mere motion can lawfully get out of the Union; that resolves and ordinances to that effect are legally void, and that acts of violence within any State or States against the authority of the United States are insurrectionary or revolutionary, according to circumstances.

"I therefore consider that in view of the Constitution and the laws the Union is unbroken, and to the extent of my ability, I shall take care, as the Constitution itself expressly enjoins upon me, that the laws of the Union be faithfully executed in all the States. Doing this I deem to be only a simple duty on my part, and I shall perform it so far as practicable unless my rightful masters, the American people, shall withhold the requisite means or in some authoritative manner direct the contrary. I trust this will not be regarded as a menace, but only as the declared purpose of the Union that it will constitutionally defend and maintain itself."

Six hundred thousand lives were sacrificed in the Civil War to preserve and defend the cause of the perpetuity of the Union. In addition to the sacrifices made by the soldiers in the fields, much of this immense toll was born by the families of the soldiers who died on both sides. It was for these reasons that Lincoln eloquently expressed his desire for restoration with compassion in the closing words of his Second Inaugural Address: "With malice toward none; with charity for all; with firmness in the right, as God gives us to see the right, let us strive on to finish the work we are in; to bind up the nation's wounds; to care for him who shall have borne the battle, and for his widow, and his orphan—to do all which may achieve and cherish a just, and a lasting peace, among ourselves, and with all nations."

Excerpt from the Emancipation Proclamation, Abraham Lincoln, January 1, 1863, Washington, D.C.

The second great cause to which Lincoln was dedicated was freedom for all men. As noted, this was his personal wish but it became a proclamation of war as well. The Emancipation Proclamation, written in September of 1862, was implemented on January 1, 1863. It was a humanitarian measure on one level, but wholly constructed on the other as a war measure to help assure a Union victory.

Note these words from the document: "Now, therefore I, Abraham Lincoln, President of the United States, by virtue of the power in me vested as Commander-in-Chief, of the Army and Navy of the United States in time of actual armed rebellion against the authority and government of the United States, and as a fit and necessary war measure for suppressing said rebellion, do, on this first day of January, in the year of our Lord one thousand eight hundred and sixty-three, and in accordance with my purpose so to do publicly proclaimed for the full period of one hundred days, from the day first above mentioned, order and designate as the States and parts of States wherein the people thereof respectively, are this day in rebellion against the United States, the following, to wit:

"Arkansas, Texas, Louisiana, (except the Parishes of St. Bernard, Plaquemines, Jefferson, St. John, St. Charles, St. James Ascension, Assumption, Terrebonne, Lafourche, St. Mary, St. Martin, and Orleans, including the City of New Orleans) Mississippi, Alabama, Florida, Georgia, South Carolina, North Carolina, and Virginia, (except the forty-eight counties designated as West Virginia, and also the counties of Berkley, Accomac, Northampton, Elizabeth City, York, Princess Ann, and Norfolk, including the cities of Norfolk and Portsmouth[)], and which excepted parts, are for the present, left precisely as if this proclamation were not issued.

"And by virtue of the power, and for the purpose aforesaid, I do order and declare that all persons held as slaves within said designated States, and parts of States, are, and henceforward shall be free; and that the Executive government of the United States, including the military and naval authorities thereof, will recognize and maintain the freedom of said persons."

Preserving one great cause may often require the execution and implementation of another where it can be shown that a leader must do both to achieve either one. This was the case here.

Enduring leadership welcomes the responsibility to preserve and defend great causes. Ask yourself, "What are those higher motives and results I am convinced are worthy of such merit that I would lead others to accomplish them even at great cost and sacrifice to myself and those I lead?"

How convinced are you of the validity of what you have learned? How well do you see that what you have been taught has shaped your belief system and worldview, and how much do you embrace earning the responsibility that comes with strong conviction based on verified and lasting truth?

List your great causes and rally your followers to them. When you do, you will reaffirm the truth of the next chapter: Words and Deeds Must Prove Each Other.

Lesson 6
Words and Deeds Must Prove Each Other

Closely aligned with preserving and defending great causes is the effective leader's recognition that the leader's words and deeds will intersect because they must. In fact, there are no alternatives to this truth.

There may be instances where words of a leader are not proven by actions readily, but eventually actions will follow words if what is declared is uttered with integrity and an honest and resolute intention of follow-through. Actions prove what words require when words emerge from an honest leader who owns not only what he or she says, but what he or she does.

Followers who want to learn will investigate on their own while they look to their leaders to point the way, give instruction, and model desired behaviors. As stated in *Lessons of War*, page 28: "Eager inquirers' desires for knowledge run deep. They study the words and deeds of leaders thoroughly, yearning to know how they intersected."

The importance of this model of intersection of words and deeds cannot be overstated. At the very least, it should consistently be remembered. Consider that in situations where a leader's words and deeds don't match, that leader's credibility is severely undermined if not dismissed. This outcome is not unusual, nor should it be.

Declaration

There is great value in declaration. Declaring what is wanted puts the leader in prime position to set the processes in place that will achieve the goal. Declaration is the first step toward dedicated action on the parts of the leader and follower; in fact, action not first declared as to intent may seem out of place, unrealistic, or burdensome. When followers simply don't know what is wanted or what inspired or drove the leader to make the choices the leader made, it is far more difficult for the follower to achieve full buy-in.

Leaders who want their followers to fully understand what is desired disclose reasons, right activities, and responsible duties. Clarity within these discussions births understanding and commitment to closure from those who follow as a natural outgrowth.

Clarity and Closure

Clarity defines the issue, project, or action, and designs the course of action for its accomplishment. Closure performs the duties and informs the leader of completion of the job (see *Core Teams Work Their Principles and Practices*, page 97, www.CoreTeamsWork.com). Where a leader's words are clear, closure has the best chance of occurring from dedicated core team members.

Jack was the CEO of a mid-sized company. He was fond of making commitments that either he couldn't keep or decided not to follow through on. When followers of any rank expressed their dissatisfaction with his lack of performance his excuses ranged from "I forgot" to "I changed my mind" to "It's no concern of yours" or "I checked with other leaders and we can't go forward." The excuse barrage didn't happen occasionally. It was repeated time and again. It was frustrating to those he oversaw. It was also the eventual reason his followers went to the company's Board of Directors and exposed the recurring problems that had produced such enormous discontent and disconnect. This exposure led, rightfully, to the dismissal of this CEO. Even more interesting, when the CEO was departing, he told many of his closest employees, "You should have done this a long time ago." In this, he was right.

Effective leadership doesn't buy time with meaningless words. Great leaders don't promise something they can't deliver, and they will not try to inspire followers on the basis of hope without substance. Instead, true leaders engender loyalty with truth, words with appropriate deeds, and promises with timely and responsible fulfillment. True and honest leadership states what is wanted and acts upon what is said.

Excerpt from the Gettysburg Address, Abraham Lincoln, November 19, 1863, Gettysburg, Pennsylvania

The Gettysburg Address is composed of 267 words. Within this brief speech Lincoln made some observations from history that most people know very well. As he closed the speech he projected central and abiding truths that were germane to the future reunification of the country as it became "the Union as it was." Note these concluding sentences:

"It is for us the living, rather, to be dedicated here to the unfinished work which they who fought here have thus far so nobly advanced. It is rather for us to be here dedicated to the great task remaining before us—that from these honored dead we take increased devotion to that cause for which they gave the last full measure of devotion—that we here highly resolve that these dead shall not have died in vain—that this nation, under God, shall have a new birth of freedom—and that government of the people, by the people, for the people, shall not perish from the earth."

Lincoln adroitly and candidly tied these elements together for his audience and for those who would read the speech later:

1. The unfinished work of winning a conflict: the dedication to completion of the great task before him and those he led
2. The nobility of a higher cause
3. The ultimate sacrifice on the part of all participants
4. A firm resolve: that nothing should dissuade committed people from accomplishing their courses
5. Completion of responsibility seen in ultimate restoration of the Union

The central focus, of course, was the perpetuity of a country that was the creation of, by, and for its own people. Clarity was paramount; indeed, his conciseness of thought and presentation endeared the speech for all time as well as became foundational for the fulfillment of its goals.

But it wasn't just the speech. It was what came after it, spread over two additional years of bloody conflict that bore the fruit of the words so eloquently spoken. Lincoln saw what had to be done even though he and no one else could have known at the time of the delivery of the speech the immense degrees of sacrifice both the North and South would endure.

The war didn't come to an end until 1865, but Lincoln was immovably convinced that ultimate victory for the Union was the *only* way that his words could produce more than lofty concepts beautifully expressed. Deeds had to follow these words, regardless of costs, if anything of permanence was to be achieved.

When a leader does not follow words with deeds, instability and confusion are often the predictable results on the inside along with a lack of completed tasks and unhappy customers on the outside. Instability like this occurs in any form of organization, be it government or private sector, for-profit or non-profit where ineffective leadership speaks but does not act.

Dale is a religious man. He is also the leader, or "senior pastor" of a large and growing church in a major cosmopolitan city. He is a big-vision thinker and in public demonstrates a boisterous and contagiously inviting personality. He often "makes fun of himself" to endear himself to his followers. This tactic works to a point, but at some levels it also breeds doubt and a growing loss of confidence in Dale's apparent competence.

Of course, there is nothing wrong with big vision. There is also nothing wrong with "out in front" personality displays. There may be some concern in showing too much self deprecation, but those aren't the primary issues. The big problem comes when Dale speaks before he fully thinks through what he is going to say—and he does it a lot—in fact, way too much. Perhaps this is a demonstration of the true core issue: a gross insecurity within himself.

Much damage is done, repeatedly, as followers who think he is in touch "with God's plan," try to follow and fulfill what Dale expresses he wants, only to be cut off at the next opportunity when he suddenly changes his course regardless of the reasons, discarding former plans and the people who had tried to help his original ideas come to fruition. It's a roller coaster for the people who try to help his vision become reality, and people often get sick when riding a rollercoaster too much.

The frustration at Dale's church is rampant. Many effective team and staff members have departed, and many are contemplating leaving. Why? Because Dale often does not mean what he says, or say what he means. Some staff and parishioners have even accused him of out-and-out deception when he is caught in what appear and are proven to be misleading comments about dreams, dictates, and demands for fulfillment. His words, far too often, have been proven to be misstatements or even lies.

As one recently departed high-ranking staff member put it, "Working with him is like trying to drink water from a fire hydrant: a dump truck load of words with almost no commitment for completion of any task, and a really big mess that others have to clean up when the spills and spoils are spread out everywhere."

Great leadership is far more secure than this. It articulates the courses required to complete the worthy goals at hand, and does so *with full intent and commitment to follow through because enough self confidence exists to do so*. This superior leadership guides its followers to embody those courses with action, to produce desired outcomes, and doesn't change courses regularly because original ideas and dictates were not thoroughly thought through from the beginning.

If you are the leader, check your words. Begin by checking your motives. What you say probably has tremendous impact. If you say it, make sure you believe and are committed to it—

make sure you are expressing the truth and are dedicated to fulfilling it.

When you combine carefully constructed words with deeds that match, you will chart a course of clarity and closure for your followers that they desperately need. Plus, you will provide a path of completion for your organization that will sustain it into its future.

Lesson 7
Enduring Leadership Principles Live for All Time

In unstable business environments, usually seen in shaky economic markets, people rightfully look for something that lasts. In the Great Recession that most people believe began in 2007, thousands of people (many in companies served by CTRG, so we possess this knowledge first hand) have lost their jobs. They have also been deprived of a lifetime of retirement funds from stock market downturns, business bankruptcies, and government takeovers. It has been one of the ugliest and most descriptive pictures of instability since the Great Depression.

Those who remember the Great Depression are aghast when they realize the hardships on business leaders of this early 21st Century—and they have good reason for their concerns. One of the biggest problems that continues to feed the recession is mounting and out of control government debt.

According to several sources, the National Debt of the United States in April of 2012 stood more than halfway between *15 trillion* and *16 trillion* dollars, climbing at the rate of approximately $300,000.00 *per minute.* It is a figure most people cannot even begin to grasp. Put into more understandable terms, based on a population of about 300 million in the U.S., each person's "share" of this astronomical number is more than $50,000.00. Perhaps even more astounding, according to many sources, the amount of national debt, as of this writing, continues to climb at the rate of nearly *$4 billion per day.*

To speak of the United States as fiscally stable when the country is awash in this much financial mismanagement, is a contradiction. The methods any Congress and any administration develop and utilize to begin to tackle and solve the debt crisis will and must belong to leadership in the House, Senate, and office of the President, those people who are supposed to be committed to benefitting the country, not simply keeping their jobs and growing and retaining power. The country *can* conquer its debt demon but not without policies that give tax relief and thereby more discretionary income to private enterprise and small businesses, which in turn empowers these entities to hire more people, develop more profitable business partnerships, and bring back the chance for fiscal stability to the vast majority of Americans who desire to contribute to their family's health and the nation's wealth.

In an environment of this kind, is it any wonder that people want something that lasts? Is it any wonder they feel threatened nearly to the point of resignation when because of government intrusion, gross mismanagement, and bureaucratic bungling a lifetime of careful planning and saving can be wiped out because of overbearing controls or taxation run amuck?

In early 2012 I received a call from a gold investing firm. According to many people, that commodity is the *only* hedge against monetary fiascos during a recessionary struggle. "Will this ever end?" I inquired this of the gold investment sales person. His answer was what all of us know, "I don't know." Then he went on to praise the value of gold as a hedge against loss, as you would expect.

Whether the recession will end or when it will end if it does, one truth remains: it will never cease unless leaders are elected who care more about the country than they do about themselves. Part of a great leader's promise is to the people they serve, not their personal pockets they seek to fill. This means that those leaders will honor the Declaration of Independence and the Constitution of the United States, the documents that at their cores sought to protect the citizen from overbearing government controls. For the government to assist the country, it simply needs to get out of the way, lessen the tax burden, and stimulate economic growth through means *other than borrowing*. Putting money back into the economy is best accomplished by freeing those who want to invest, to invest more because they have the money to invest—money that has not been stolen through excessive taxation by a government hell-bent on borrowing and printing more money and telling its citizens how to spend it.

And herein is the lesson. From *Lessons of War*, page 29: "Strong leadership principles emerge in a study of this kind. An abiding appreciation of history, a long-term vision for generations yet unborn, bold strategies of winning over an enemy, resolving conflict between former combatants, ultimate sacrifices and requirements of duty, tough decision making, and clear communication are a few of them… Enduring lessons of leadership live for all time. They outlast conflict because they encompass eternal and uplifting values. These principles when applied empower a warrior [or any committed patriot] to face virtually any challenge with right motives and honorable deeds. Effective leaders rest their choices of action on truths that abide when called upon to make momentous decisions and follow through."

Let's break it down. First, consider an abiding appreciation of history which teaches that no nation can tax itself into wealth. The more confiscatory taxes that are imposed the smaller the opportunity becomes for any economy to survive.

Second, a long-term vision for generations yet unborn must take into account what kind of economic environment is being created for the people of today *and* tomorrow. When I stop and think that upon birth my grandchildren each one is *already* saddled with upwards of $50,000.00 of government debt, the thought is sickening.

Next, please ask: "What are the bold strategies of winning over an enemy?" No strategy for winning can exist until first the enemy is identified for what it is. Let's describe the debt as the "enemy." If the debt is the enemy, then how can it be conquered? There are several strategies. Of primary importance: "Don't spend more than you take in." Another: "Live slightly below your means." Still another: "Buy little or nothing of depreciating value on credit. If you don't have the money, don't spend any money you don't have." And still one more: "If you must leverage debt, do so only on appreciating assets." Oh, and let's not forget this one: "Pay off debt and balance the budget." Consider the positive results that most would enjoy were these truths to be applied over the next twenty to thirty years of economic life in the United States. Frankly, the fact that the Democrat-controlled Senate of the United States did not put forth a budget in over three years as of 2012 is deplorable.

One principle of leadership emerges that Lincoln espoused in the closing of his Second Inaugural Address. It is this: "With malice toward none…" Malice is a word that often describes premeditated destruction fostered upon someone else. Arguments and debates, even heated ones as to policy and procedure should take place in a free society, but respect for the law and the dignity of each person must remain as firm foundations for disagreements even if these disagreements become conflictive. Health occurs when more than one opinion is discussed and debated. Healing occurs when former combatants choose to live according to the rule of law as established by the majority of voters in an honest election.

A call to duty to uphold the law, or rightfully change the laws that are deemed no longer to be valid, is the call of every American citizen who cherishes freedom. This kind of commitment often calls for more than average commitment; it may mean sacrifice on many levels. Strong belief exercised within the constraints of law and liberty becomes the impetus for positive change and uplifting results. The strength of decisions and choices based on enduring principles is in graphic evidence when *a leader shows how it's done by doing it first* and when that leader *lives by the principles that are espoused in the founding documents.*

Leaders who are positive life-changers on behalf of those they lead must accept that enduring principles existed before they did and will outlive them. One of those principles is freedom. It's both freedom *from* tyranny and freedom among many *toward* profitable enterprise. It is incumbent on leaders who wish to make lasting and humanely beneficial contributions to align with the principles that have been shown to be true, communicate them effectively, and live them unreservedly. "Fairness" is not one of the freedoms granted in the founding documents. While compassion must be a part of human endeavor, and we should help those who cannot help themselves, it is wrong for any government to decide who gets what when that decision robs the individual who wants to earn and yearns to make a positive difference of his or her right to life, liberty, and the pursuit of happiness within the law.

Perfection here is not the goal because it can't be. However, perseverance of right action based on enduring truth is the goal because it must be. Great leadership knows this, as Lincoln did, and embraces it.

That kind of leadership changes circumstances and alters history. While Lincoln did not live to see the true end of the Civil War or to see slavery officially abolished, he gave his entire presidency to the belief that the causes were worth the fight, the sacrifice, and the struggle to assure that the United States would endure for all time, much like the principles of human equality and the rights to life, liberty, and the pursuit of happiness upon which the nation was founded in the first place. In this leadership he succeeded and the country was better for it then, and it still is better for it now in spite of its fiscal duress.

If you are the leader, consider the principles that you embrace, the ones you know are right and true because they have been proven so. Which ones will mark you, and which ones will you incorporate as part of your contribution of leadership to those who follow you?

Perhaps you will be one of the leaders who will take up the challenge to unselfishly move the nation back toward living in an environment of less debt and more economic freedom where people can have and enjoy the ability to invest in themselves and others and in the country they love. If that's you, then don't wait; get started. Make a difference!

Lesson 8
Learning Becomes Living
When Behaviors Change

There is a huge difference between learning and living. Learning occurs when knowledge is taught and received. Living occurs when that knowledge is turned into changes of behavior. It is only when behaviors change that learning becomes more than information.

Too often leaders stop short. They may acquire information and teach their teams or followers what they have received, but they may not expect, provide for, coach, or model for the teams *how* behaviors must change to make learning and application endure. Further, leaders stop short when they fail to provide action and communication loop closure that includes proper reporting, evaluation, correction, and celebration *by doing it first, themselves.*

Lincoln was a master at requiring changes of behavior within him as well as others, to accomplish lasting change. One example revolves around the Emancipation Proclamation, a war and humanitarian measure that went into effect on January 1, 1863 as noted in Lesson 5. Lincoln had crafted the document several months prior and then agreed that a Union victory was needed before the proclamation could be issued. This "waiting until the proper time" was done to assure that the measure didn't appear to be a move born of desperation from a losing side. That victory came, or some would say barely came tactically at least, at Antietam or Sharpsburg in Maryland, on September 17, 1862. Five days later Lincoln issued the preliminary proclamation declaring that on January 1, 1863 its provisions would be enacted.

Lincoln was a diligent learner who put his knowledge and beliefs into action. There was no doubt that Lincoln desired all men to be free; his public addresses had noted his preference and desire for many years, in fact, since 1837. He also knew as the war progressed through 1861 and 1862 that the Emancipation Proclamation would free up manpower to fight for the Union.

The 13th Amendment to the Constitution of the United States

However, events were partially the masters here. Certain military milestones had to be achieved for the Emancipation Proclamation to have its greatest effect and prepare the nation, once its national unity was restored, to eventually outlaw slavery with the 13th Amendment to the Constitution of the United States. That amendment was enacted on December 6, 1865—many months after Lincoln had been assassinated. The text reads as follows:

> **Section 1.** Neither slavery nor involuntary servitude, except as a punishment for crime whereof the party shall have been duly convicted, shall exist within the United States, or any place subject to their jurisdiction.
>
> **Section 2.** Congress shall have power to enforce this article by appropriate legislation.

Had Lincoln not allowed events to take their course and enacted the proclamation when he did, results could have turned out much differently. It took more than learning that slavery was wrong to actually eradicate slavery from the United States.

This learning and belief of Lincoln had taken 28 years, a Civil War, the capitulation of Robert E. Lee and the Army of Northern Virginia to Ulysses S. Grant at Appomattox, several additional Union victories that followed that momentous event, and Lincoln's assassination before slavery finally was abolished by an amendment to the Constitution.

Lincoln's strong belief was one he had proclaimed often to those who heard him. But learning information which led to the formation of belief, both Lincoln's and that of the people he influenced, did not become action until a vote in 1865 reflected the behaviors of the people who passed the legislation and changed the behaviors of an entire country that for over a hundred years had tolerated, encouraged, and in some respects depended on slavery as a part of its economic and social existence.

Changing Behavior

How strong does learning become when it gives birth to action? Put these questions into the perspective of your environment. Ask yourself, "What are the changes that I would like to see accomplished in my work world?" "How will I teach, or instruct what I want, and how will learning occur on the parts of those whose tasks will become to actuate what they have been taught?" If they learn, and even agree with what you want but *don't act* on that knowledge and belief, nothing will change. Thought processes surrounding some good ideas can bounce around endlessly and if they remain in the mind they don't produce positive change. Only action from people willing and wanting to alter their behaviors produces positive change.

The leader's job is to communicate fully what is desired and then create pathways for action to follow that will cause change to occur and abide, setting the model in place of what is desired through the behaviors the leader changes within him or herself, first.

There's the rub and the reason that just because information is received and taught there is no guarantee that anything will happen. In fact, unless *someone* changes his or her behavior by literally *doing it differently according to the dictates agreed upon and the effects desired on the other end* no lasting benefits will be realized.

Dreams and great ideas remain within the mind unless the heart and hand cooperate to fulfill what is desired. Leader and follower who agree that uplifting change is needed based on abiding principle, who learn what they must, who articulate their desires for changes clearly and then *do them* are those who prove the truth that learning becomes living only when behaviors change.

Some truths are worth articulating and fighting for. The abolition of slavery in the United States is a primary example. It is incumbent upon a leader to decide what positive alterations are needed in his or her contemporary environment, teach them to the followers, assure that knowledge is received, agreement is obtained, and then *act, and show others by their instruction and modeling how to act.* Then and only then will change occur and be sustained.

Lesson 9
Frameworks, Followers, and Fulfillment

Place yourself in the position of one who is retained to do a job about which you do not have enough information to allow you to complete your task well. Training is required, and in most environments adequate training may be offered and received. That alone may seem to be sufficient on one level, but in the context of a healthy team composed of solid leadership and committed following, much more is required because much more is at stake.

A Framework of Success: Teaching, Modeling, Encouragement, and Support

Leadership is about setting a framework for success for the follower. I define leadership success as "seeing another person fulfill their dreams and goals with the leader's teaching, modeling, encouragement, and support." (*Leadership Is—How to Build Your Legacy* Revised Version, © 2012, page 16.) When a leader provides a follower with teaching, modeling, encouragement, and support, a framework is constructed in which a follower can succeed if the follower really wants to.

Lincoln sought to build a superb framework of governing when he began to serve out his administration in 1861. Students of Lincoln are aware that the cabinet of individuals Lincoln first assembled was largely composed of the people who had run against him. On one hand, it made perfect sense—sort of. These men, apparently, were the best and brightest, so why wouldn't Lincoln choose them to serve in his administration?

On the other hand his choice would truly concern anyone who was not extremely secure in their understanding of their own personal strengths, including firmly held beliefs and practices, and their abilities to lead others. Lincoln knew or came to know that anytime men with grandiose ideas, strong personalities, and accompanying egos serve together, sparks and fires are bound to result. And they did, even though it is repeatedly told that Lincoln referred to his first cabinet as his "Happy Family." You can almost see him smile as he says it, can't you?

Regardless, the governing group that Lincoln constructed was founded on much more than the potential for sparks to fly. It certainly was not dependent on whether or not those people "got along" all the time. That group with its attending responsibilities was built upon the president's desire to bring together gifted individuals for the cause of the preservation of the Union. In this there had to be unadulterated agreement, and there was.

Frameworks of Lasting Principles and Commitments

Leaders with a long and enduring view of success set frameworks in place on the basis of lasting principles along with the commitments to fulfilling great causes. These are the frameworks in which followers will position themselves to affect the greatest good for the leader they serve and the purposes they are called to achieve.

As the events unfolded on the tragic day of September 11, 2001, the country united. The United States demonstrated firm and unshakable commitment to solidarity in the crisis, not only in expressing its grief but in its decision and dedication to right a horrible and unjustifiable wrong. Who can forget the members of Congress assembling on the steps of the Capital singing "God Bless America" to show the country their oneness and resolve? There were no party affiliations that day; all were Americans and all were united to survive and bring to justice the perpetrators of the cowardly and extremely costly act of war.

It took ten years but Osama bin Laden was killed in 2011 under the administration of President Obama. Two prior presidents, Bill Clinton and George W. Bush had also tried to eliminate him. By the time of Osama bin Laden's death, Al Qaida had already experienced the deserved loss of many of its top radical Islamic and terrorist military leaders. That demonic organization will continue to be vanquished because America will never forget 911.

A framework in which followers position themselves is one that is crafted by leaders on behalf of the operations and successes of their followers. A leader's job is to define the parameters of success, provide the tools to accomplish it, and support the followers as they fulfill the tasks for which they are retained.

If a team falters in its methods, one reason may be that a framework for success has not been firmly constructed. It's far more than a commitment to duty on the part of the follower who wants to grow and contribute. The commitment of the follower must include his or her leader's *teaching, modeling, encouragement,* and *support*. A breakout of these action terms is important.

Teaching is the first goal of any leader who wants to establish a framework of success for a follower. Little is or can be assumed; instruction must be birthed in principle and practice, and a follower must position him or herself as a student even as his or her leader also remains a student, for a great leader remains a committed follower, and an excellent teacher remains a committed student. The desire to learn must never go away.

Modeling is a term that simply means that the leader shows *how* it is done through example in word and deed. The model the leader creates becomes the essential template for the follower to emulate in attitude and action.

Encouragement is more than cheerleading, although it can encompass this. Encouragement is the reassurance, again in word and deed often coming from direct experience that the leader understands and actively promotes the follower's growth. In a healthy leader-follower engagement, encouragement is constantly done. It must be present and active in a well built framework for success. Encouragement is best accomplished from leader to follower when the leader can truly say, "I've been where you are or know others who have, and I know how you feel, what you are going through, the challenges you face, and the victories you'll win." Nothing speaks truth louder than a convincing proof of experience where the leader can say, "I did it. You can do it, too."

In *Leadership Is—How to Build Your Legacy* Revised Version © 2012, pages 225-228, a point is made about this term *support*, comparing it to *nurture*. Support is help from the inside out, while nurture is assistance from the outside in. Support certainly feels better, and both are often required in a healthy leader-follower relationship. But without support, an entire framework of investment can collapse. Put another way, leaders can be great coaches when they've experienced the game, because they have been where the players are and understand fully the means and meaning of winning and losing.

A leader supports best when the follower and leader identify with each other's interests, and communication flows freely between them. This arrangement works because they work it!

A framework for success founded upon teaching, modeling, encouragement, and support will provide what both leader and follower need to succeed. Success can occur in spite of personality differences, aggressive egos, divergent views, pressing problems now, and the crises that are sure to come.

Build a framework like this on behalf of those who work for you. Then work within it to help assure the success of those who look to you for leadership.

Lesson 10

Truth Wins Because It Must

"Principles of leadership endure because they are true. They are repeatable and therefore should be repeated. When enacted from right motives they produce positive and enduring results regardless of degrees of negativity and controversy, the time required to see results come to fruition, or the immensity of sacrifice involved. Truth wins eventually because it must." (*Lessons of War*, page 32)

Great Leadership Regenerates Itself

Perhaps the single most overlooked piece of the evidence of great leadership is that when it is truly great it regenerates itself into the lives and activities of followers who become leaders, and this regeneration creates exponential returns. Followers not only become superb leaders; they accomplish more than their original leaders could ever do!

Leadership like this is not an anomaly; it's a realistic expectation *if* the leadership is really done well from the right motives and with the right methods and *if* the leadership is more concerned with building beyond the immediate for results that outlast the current leader.

Conversely, poor leadership doesn't strive to regenerate itself into the lives of followers; in fact, it often tries to stifle the growth of those who follow because at its core it wallows in insecurity and therefore resides on shaky ground. Less than adequate and therefore ineffective leadership often dwells in falsehood, mistrust, pitting followers against one another, and disingenuous and hidden agendas revealed mostly in undermining gossip that puts other people down behind their backs. Rarely if ever does leadership like this want to live in truth; in fact, staying hidden and subversive is the goal of a leader who exercises these behaviors. Sometimes despicable acts are performed by these kinds of leaders under a guise of superiority but usually they are simply ugly demonstrations of a gross lack of confidence, weakness, mistrust, and contempt.

Unfortunately, poor leadership like this is what too many followers experience too often, regardless of the work environment. Let's face it: where these kinds of leadership demonstrations are prevalent, unadulterated truth is neither being told nor lived.

People who are leaders, or who call themselves leaders who act poorly have choices if they want to improve. First, they admit their inadequacies, ask for help, and seek to mature. Then they practice the kinds of leadership that endure and produce positive results. Easy? No. Worth it? Yes, especially if a poor leader wants to become rich in the investment he or she makes into and with his or her followers.

Sam was brought in to head a well known and apparently successful firm after its twenty year anniversary. He had been acquired after a national search that consumed seven months. The teams already in place at the firm were functional, but lethargy had begun to set in amongst the employees because innovation hadn't been on the forefront as time had ticked by. Sales were lagging. Emotions were in neutral, and a general sense of entitlement had started to rob the company of its competitive edge.

While the organization from its inception had met the growing needs and demands of a vibrant customer population, times had changed and the company hadn't changed with them. The company had drifted into autopilot mode.

Sam appeared to be a breath of fresh air, an invigorating force that would re-stimulate the cause and the course. He was exuberant and his enthusiasm contagious. He voiced strong opinions and innovative ideas. His very presence commanded respect. His public presentations were highly motivational and heartwarming. His past experiences appeared to be the ones the company felt would help them in their time of need, so his entrance into the organization as the new CEO was made with welcome arms, open attitudes, and an awful lot of hoopla.

Sam had been a consummate success and it looked like success would follow him anywhere. All the trappings of "better times to come under his leadership" were present.

His first year was a smashing success. People loved him. Profits were up. The company's name and standing was growing. Two more years went by. More profits went up. Sales territories expanded. Product lines increased. Innovation in marketing and advertising brought in stronger sales numbers, some at levels only dreamt of before Sam's arrival—if they had even been imagined.

A part of Sam's operational paradigm was to surround himself with competent leaders and managers, usually a characteristic of secure and effective leadership. The casual observer would conclude that Sam had chosen the right and strongest folks to run the company with him—the best of the best that the firm could afford. From this pool, over time, Sam formed an inner core of top executives and managers who heard from the outset how important loyalty to Sam really was, and that the culture Sam desired was one of unreserved dedication to his leadership. That devotion factor to Sam's leadership became part of the DNA, a necessary requirement of this top leadership team.

Upon their entrance each member of that group declared their loyalty—to Sam first, above all else. That term, *loyalty* became the by-word of this top tier of leaders. To them, loyalty to Sam was *it*. They never questioned it. They always talked about it, projected it, and promoted it through the ranks.

If anyone of that group ever doubted, questioned, or got too close to probing what made Sam tick, he or she was subjected to the interrogations in front of Sam that usually centered on questions like, "Can we trust you?" along with accusations of violating trust in the top guy. A degree of "failure" permeated meetings where loyalty was questioned or worse yet, investigated. These scenes were ugly when they happened, and over time they started to happen more and more often.

This environment was built upon itself. Much more was assumed than ever should have been. Excuses for "under the table" dealings and "behind the scenes" maneuvering were heard after awhile as it was revealed that Sam had done some things that smacked of subversion, perhaps illegality, but nothing could be proven. This was especially true in financial dealings: reporting of income and investments, utilizing funds from other interested parties to fund expanding interests.

Webs of financial networking expanded under Sam's watch and with them more and more information became not readily available. Sam was adept at hiding information when he needed to, and he began to falsify or not disclose information (though no one knew or could prove it at the time) at an alarming rate.

Soon this house of cards began to topple. The first indication to the outside observer that all was not well was when Sam tried to overtly manipulate the markets to increase his sales, and was reprimanded by the authorities for doing so. He struck a deal a government agency that had become concerned. Sam defended his position: supposedly "it was everyone else's fault." Validation came from a case against Sam that eventually was thrown out of court.

But the undercurrents didn't stop. The indication that "something is wrong here" accelerated. Soon investigations occurred from media news outlets when discrepancies of financial reporting were discovered by an employee who stumbled onto financial records not put away in the company safe. Of course, that employee was terminated, but not before the proverbial can of worms was opened and opened wide. And there were many worms, many worms.

Over the course of a year the truth came to light. The bottom line was this: Sam had been embezzling funds for nearly the whole time he was employed as the CEO. Those close to him may have suspected this or something like it, maybe they had even questioned him about some of his dealings, but *loyalty* to Sam had caused them to distrust their own eyes and ears, and they simply had put the idea of Sam doing unlawful or despiteful actions away from them. It was all too hard to believe. "Sam? No, he wouldn't do that."

A District Attorney got involved and accusations flew as did multiple lawsuits. Eventually Sam was tried and convicted of multiple counts of fraud, misappropriation of funds, stealing, and money laundering. He was found guilty of lying under oath. He is in prison and will be for upwards of 25 years. The lawsuits against him will not go away and he will be paying restitution for the rest of his life.

How sad when because of perceived if not required *loyalty* to a *person* instead of the *truth* the end result destroys lives, reputations, livelihoods, and opportunities for success. The immense toll Sam caused did not involve just losses to him—the effects of this kind of thing never reside only with the perpetrator. The damage over time was revealed to touch hundreds of individuals and cost millions of dollars which most believe will never be repaid.

"Truth wins eventually because it must." (*Lessons of War*, page 32) Never was that more true than in the case of Lincoln's belief in the sacredness of the equality of every individual. The cards were stacked against the president in this regard: an entire society's welfare benefitted from enslaving others and historical precedent was in play because slavery had been around before the founding of the original Constitution.

Excerpt from the Declaration of Independence, July 4, 1776

It was true that the Declaration of Independence had declared: "We hold these truths to be self-evident, that all men are created equal, that they are endowed by their Creator with certain unalienable Rights, that among these are Life, Liberty and the pursuit of Happiness.—That to secure these rights, Governments are instituted among Men, deriving their just powers from the consent of the governed…" Lincoln, however, had correctly postulated that the framers of the Constitution had set up a system where eventually slavery would come to an end.

Those loyal to slavery had come to depend upon the institution, much like those loyal to Sam had come to depend on him to the point that questioning or opposing what was taken to be "normal" or "the way we do things here" meant a violation of what some considered a right, entitlement, or privilege. Both were wrong.

Where truth is told and honored it becomes the standard against which all other opinions must be measured. The inherent value of the individual as a person with God-given rights was a self-evident truth that, when placed alongside the loss of dignity that slavery demanded, would graphically demonstrate the truth that God's image resided within every person and that eternal truth would transcend and eventually triumph over slavery. In Sam's case, truth won because violations could not be contained or hidden forever. They never are.

Excerpt from the "House Divided" Speech, Abraham Lincoln, June 16, 1858, Springfield, Illinois

Let's revisit Lincoln's "House Divided" Speech delivered June 16, 1858 in Springfield, Illinois. Mr. Lincoln had a unique way of getting to the central point of an issue in common language, and doing so quickly. Here is what his audience heard about twenty seconds into the speech:

> We are now far into the *fifth* year, since a policy was initiated, with the *avowed* object, and *confident* promise, of putting an end to slavery agitation. Under the operation of that policy, that agitation has not only, *not ceased*, but has *constantly augmented*.
>
> In *my* opinion, it *will* not cease, until a *crisis* shall have been reached, and passed. "A house divided against itself cannot stand."
>
> I believe this government cannot endure, permanently half *slave* and half *free*.
>
> I do not expect the Union to be *dissolved*—I do not expect the house to *fall*—but I *do* expect it will cease to be divided.
>
> It will become *all* one thing or *all* the other.
>
> Either the *opponents* of slavery, will arrest the further spread of it, and place it where the public mind shall rest in the belief that it is in the course of ultimate extinction; or its *advocates* will push it

forward, till it shall become alike lawful in *all* the States, *old* as well as *new*—*North* as well as *South*.

Lincoln was correct as history would prove. A key point is this: all law should be based on abiding truth. Laws founded upon and upholding truth will be honored and practiced because they are shown unequivocally to be right.

The principle for leaders today is simple enough. Consider this question: "What laws, policies, procedures that uphold true principles have I and my organization's teams put into place?" If any are not grounded firmly on eternal principles they will eventually fall. In your organization, illustrate and promote truth through your laws and procedures. Don't try to change the truth with an opinion that may or may not be true.

Lesson 11
Recognizing Conflict

From *Lessons of War*, pages 32 and 33: "Conflict has been part of the human experience since the dawn of history. War is only one example of its presence. Opposing views and resultant action occur on many levels.

"In any conflict sides in opposition strive for what they believe is right. Compromise is possible only when one or both of the antagonists submit to the other. Compromise fails when ideologies remain too far apart, trust between people is absent, parties are immovably entrenched in their beliefs, and a willingness to consider opposing views does not exist. In these conditions the only remaining choice may be war and conquest, conditions where one side is victorious and the other vanquished."

Think of the conflicts you and your organization have faced in the last few months. Each one may be unique, but all will have illustrated similar characteristics.

For example, at CTRG we believe *every* conflict or disagreement having to do with people working together (as opposed to failures of inanimate objects like machinery or computers), regardless of degree, can be traced back to a violation of a relational principle. Think of the importance of recognizing conflict for not only what you see, but also what you don't see. Know what's behind a conflict, and you will better know how to solve it.

People Are More Important Than Production

Consider this premise: people are more important than production. Relationships (the people side) come before and give birth to function (the production side). In consideration of "people problems" these *always* begin with a violation of a relationship.

Relationship and Function

We provide specific definitions for these two important terms, *relationship* and *function*. A *relationship* is the decision I make about your success. While I can't, and shouldn't, own your success—that's for you to do—I can make decisions that support your success. A *function* or task is the action that corroborates the decision I've made. A function is the action I choose in support of the decision I made.

I can make a relationship decision about your success and do absolutely nothing to prove it. In these cases, this relationship, so-called, is nothing more than a collection of nice thoughts or intentions that never come to fruition. But when I make a decision about your success and then show it with my actions, my words are validated by my works. The cycle is completed and the process of honoring relational principles upheld. Intent is proven in deeds, not just thoughts and words.

One of the greatest ways to recognize conflict is to see where relationships have broken down and functions are being affected. Remember: relationships (decisions) always come before actions (functions). When two or more people are in conflict, they will demonstrate this at some point in their relationship. You as the leader *should* address what went wrong in the function, of course; but your *real* responsibility is to discover the relationship principle or principles that have been violated, those that led to the dysfunction in the first place.

Where dysfunction exists, a relational decision was made about someone's failure instead of a decision about his or her success, and commensurate actions followed. It's true every time in the context of negative human interaction.

Recognize that conflict is always possible where more than one person is present at the same place and time. Spend less time, however, on addressing dysfunction alone. Get to the root of the problem, the issue. There you will most likely discover the relational decisions that caused the dysfunction to occur. Address these primarily, and you've likely fixed the functional problem or are on your way to doing so.

One more word: Lincoln practiced this relationship-function principle, although he didn't frame it in those terms. It is clear, however, that as the Civil War was drawing to a close he sought to frame his actions for readmitting the States that had been in rebellion on the basis of a decision about success, the success of those States *and* the country that was being reunited. Lincoln's greatest desire was to construct a framework of renewed relationship minus subjugation and punishment ("with malice toward none…") so that within that restored framework, States coming back into the United States could once again function as they ought as part of a united country.

Lesson 12

Dealing with Conflict

Is Not Optional

From *Lessons of War*, page 49: "An organization faced with opposition studies its disagreements and carefully weighs whether conflict should be conducted. Effective leadership views the whole picture before deciding which pieces, if any, should be addressed. A leader considers the importance of impending confrontation to see if the costs of the contest and its resolution merit the fight."

Prepare for Conflict Because Conflict Is Unavoidable

From this same book on pages 34 and 35: "The question for leaders is not whether conflict occurs. The question is how they will deal with it when it comes... When faced with conflict, great leaders embrace and employ abiding principles to bring about resolution and restitution. Devoted students of history who become the leaders of their day actively use the lessons that history has proven reliable.

"If you've been a leader for any length of time you have already experienced conflict. Understand how great leaders before you handled their difficult situations and apply their practices in yours. Do what they did to produce profitable outcomes."

Beth and Roxanne had worked together only a week before the proverbial "you know what" hit the fan. Beth had hired Roxanne to be her assistant to help in the warehouse, processing orders for one of the city's premier plumbing supply companies. It was not uncommon that pressure accompanied virtually every activity of this department, from the opening minute and all through the day until after closing. The intensity of their responsibility revolved around meeting the supply demands of contractors within time schedules subject to the requirements of construction deadlines. These parameters were simply parts of "normal" operation. This was no kick-back environment—it was intense and high production, all the time, with little opportunity for pauses for refreshment.

So Beth was careful in her interviewing processes to explain carefully the nature of this operation to those who wanted to apply. She looked for a high-tolerance individual who could handle time and delivery pressures the position in the department called for.

Roxanne appeared to pass the interview with flying colors and seemed to be a person with the right temperament and tolerance ratios. To Beth it appeared that Roxanne would be a good fit; that she would contribute to the department's success. Roxanne seemed to know full well the responsibilities and requirements of a fast-paced job with extensive multi-tasking demands. In fact, bottom line, Roxanne's *function* was by all accounts going to be stellar.

Indeed, Roxanne's function appeared to be flawless in her first few days. She was a quick learner. People were impressed. Things got done, and the atmosphere, although continually charged with high demands and fast moving operations, produced higher than expected levels of customer service on a consistent basis. This kind of production efficiency helped the warehouse personnel do their jobs better and their customers were genuinely happy. This appeared to be a good combination.

But a problem began to emerge after about a month after Roxanne's start date. The issue really had nothing to do with Roxanne. It had to do with Beth. Although Beth had been instructed to "hire someone better than you" so that Beth's investment of time and energy in training and operations would prove to be worth the effort and costs, Beth suddenly found herself with an employee that was taking away (Beth thought) the prominence that Beth had enjoyed before Roxanne came.

Close to the one-month anniversary of Roxanne's hiring Beth awoke to the fact that she (Beth) was losing the spotlight. The new hire continued to hit the ball out of the park and Beth felt that the attention was now on Roxanne. Talk about green energy: Beth's focus soon became committed to planting and nourishing seeds of jealousy in her own heart; the green of envy was taking over. Jealousy started to frame Beth's relationships (decisions) and functions (actions) because she allowed if not encouraged this negativity, and soon that jealousy produced its own fruit of bitterness along with a mounting desire to "put that new employee in her place"—whatever that meant.

The end of this true story is not pretty. Beth began to make decisions about Roxanne's failure. She set her up to stumble and fall. Roxanne was given tasks that were not in line with the requirements of some particular orders and mistakes were made. These mistakes were discovered by the warehousemen and after a time they began to view Roxanne with questioning and distrusting eyes.

Roxanne noticed, of course, and was amazed. Where had she gone wrong? In instance after instance as these unfortunate events occurred she retraced her operational steps and verified that she had done exactly what Beth had communicated.

Soon the game was up. Roxanne confronted Beth in confidence and with respect, asking her why the directives given to her were inaccurate.

Beth snorted and denied it at first, but then told Roxanne a piece of the truth: that she (Beth) didn't like Roxanne's stealing the limelight in the eyes of those who had come to depend on this department's contributions.

Roxanne was shocked, disappointed, felt betrayed, and told Beth this. A rift was created that could not be bridged, and Roxanne decided that the fight wasn't worth the effort, and soon after the confrontation she left the organization. By the way, Roxanne soon landed another similar position where she worked for a far more secure leader and contributed even more than she had been able to do under Beth. In a matter of months Roxanne was promoted to head of her new department.

What had started out as functional and operational efficiency was undermined by a relational decision about someone else's failure, all because of the insecurity of a leader who felt threatened by someone else's success.

Beth didn't get the fact that great leadership *wants* followers to succeed. She didn't grasp that secure leaders are not threatened by a follower's climb to greatness. Beth's insecurity blinded her to the truth that the greatest gift any leader can give the follower is to *promote* the follower's growth because therein resides positive and reproductive legacy.

This story of relational jealousy is typical of personal conflict where the insecurity of one is confronted with the security of another. The leader with the title (Beth) didn't win when

Roxanne departed. The real leader here was Roxanne who understood that some battles were not worth the effort because the negative relational decisions and resulting dysfunctions were too great.

Roxanne's contributions to her next organization vaulted her into leadership. The differences were remarkable. Roxanne brought with her many valuable leadership lessons that included:

- Honor a leader and his or her position to the degree that you can with integrity even if you discover seeds of dysfunction.
- Continue a relentless pursuit of excellence no matter what.
- Confront relational and functional problems with truth.
- Decide if pursuing conflict is really worth the effort.
- Learn from your experience.
- Lead better because of it.
- Invest in the people you oversee and promote their progress.

From *Lincoln, Leadership and Gettysburg*, page 63: "Truths worthy of belief and sacrifice are rehearsed and applied despite pain and adverse circumstances." We know that truth wins eventually. The leader has to decide what winning is and how it will be accomplished when the cause is worth the efforts and expenditures of time, energy, money, and other resources.

Lincoln faced the most horrendous conflict imaginable in the Civil War. Truly at its outset no one could imagine what the conflict would produce in terms of human and property devastation. History has proven this.

What has to be clearly understood is that Lincoln knew from the outset what his job as President of the United States would involve, when right in front of his eyes even before his first Inauguration, the country was unraveling. Conflict had been brewing even before the repeal of the Missouri Compromise and Lincoln knew it. He also knew that as president he was the one who had to deal with it.

Farewell Speech, Abraham Lincoln, February 11, 1861, Springfield, Illinois

Lincoln had already accepted his responsibility as he said farewell to his friends and colleagues in Springfield on February 11, 1861. He gave a short speech from the train platform just before the train departed for Washington. In its words we can see how his perspective then included the past, present and future. As he viewed immense contemporary difficulties he chose a balanced approach, one that a great leader should take when embarking on a new and challenging task.

While there are several variations of this short speech, this version is one that is generally accepted as accurate. Particularly note the line where he says his task that was "greater" than Washington's:

> My friends, no one, not in my situation, can appreciate my feeling of sadness at this parting. To this place, and the kindness of these people, I owe everything. Here I have lived a quarter of a century, and have passed from a young to an old man. Here my children have been born, and one is buried.
>
> I now leave, not knowing when, or whether ever, I may return, with a task before me greater than that which rested upon Washington. Without the assistance of the Divine Being who ever attended

him, I cannot succeed. With that assistance I cannot fail.

Trusting in Him who can go with me, and remain with you, and be everywhere for good, let us confidently hope that all will yet be well. To His care commending you, as I hope in your prayers you will commend me, I bid you an affectionate farewell.

Lincoln's words illustrated a profound truth: leaders must recognize trends of dysfunction and anticipate conflict as they prepare to deal with the future. Specific elements of a conflict may take them by surprise but the big picture usually is accompanied by warning signs: an argument is brewing and something will eventually need to be done to address the issues and the incidents.

Take these truths to heart: conflict is unavoidable. It's coming if it's not already here. The leader's job is to prepare for it, address the incidents and issues, and then decide if winning is really the best course.

Where the decision to win is shown to be the right one then that choice means that every resource available is brought to bear upon achieving that goal. Such was the case in Lincoln's desire to reunite the country.

Where conflicts are shown not to be worth the expenditure of human endeavor and resources, sometimes the best course is to leave the destructive environment and go to another opportunity where the chance of employing greater leadership and building legacy is enhanced if not encouraged.

Truth wins in all cases. Choose to handle conflict well.

Lesson 13

How Strong Is Your Belief in Positive Results?

From *Lessons of War*, page 36: "If you are the leader, inquire of yourself: 'How strong is my belief? In what ways does my leadership bring about positive results?' Great leaders ask these questions, deploy their answers in their circumstances, and seek to discover improved methods of waging, winning, and ending difficult engagements.

"Lincoln's leadership held the country together even through war. In his Second Inaugural Address the president revealed how to conclude war and reconcile combatants. Leaders learn these truths and apply them where similar results are desired.

"Perhaps in your leadership you are duty-bound to hold your group together despite immense difficulties now. Lincoln sought peaceful resolution upon the conclusion of one of the greatest conflicts the world had ever known. What kind of peaceful end will you try to create in your situation?"

The forces that tend to pull people apart are not stronger than the forces that are designed to keep them together. However, within many business enterprises disconnect occurs between team members simply because some people are not committed to making decisions about each other's success. Plus, even if they do make decisions about someone's success, they may not act to prove their decisions.

Without a firm dedication toward building up other members of the team, positive results long desired may become those that simply don't occur. With a firm dedication to build up other team members, positive results earnestly desired can indeed come to fruition but only if someone *takes action* to make those desires become reality.

Commitment to Success Is Shown in Action

If I am the leader and I am committed to your success, I will show this through my actions. There is no other way. I will alter my behavior to form a framework of achievement for you, so that you can accomplish improved results and grow in your personal and professional success. It works *because we both want the same thing*. It doesn't work if we don't.

As a leader, the strength of my belief in the success of my followers and the growth of my company are directly tied to the decisions I make about their successes. There is no wiggle room here.

I may *say* I want positive results, but if my behavior does not change to promote the results I want, then my words will likely fall flat and my followers will discredit my leadership, and they won't be given the opportunity to convince themselves that I really meant it.

It all begins with the leader. In most instances, nothing of significance changes until the leader changes, first. There may be surface improvements tied to technical or operational efficiency training, and there may be positive circumstances that promote good feelings among members of the team. But these are fleeting when compared to lasting change that comes from superior choices.

Sustainable Change

What is required for *sustainable* positive results are changes desired, not necessarily required. In other words, if I as the leader really *want* improvements, I will initiate change within *my* actions to begin them. I will model for my followers the belief I proclaim and my followers will see it and emulate it because I have changed, first.

A leader who wants sustainable positive results *never* requires these of his or her followers in advance of promising and fulfilling positive change within the leader initially. For sustainable change to occur, the leader sets the pace and puts decisions and actions in place that prove the strength of belief that positive outcomes can be achieved.

Gerard led a growing business entity that provided industry-standard audio/visual production products and services to convention and community centers, local governments, theaters, churches, schools (elementary, middle schools, high schools, colleges and universities) and other groups that regularly held public events. His company's products consisted of staging, lighting, audio, and video gear—a vast array of equipment. His company's services included virtually all aspects of running the often complex technical sides of events with professional crews who were assembled to work specific productions. Committed people composed his staff and their jobs were to assure that the production side of any event was done on time, on budget, and with excellence.

Gerard himself was a consummate professional when it came to knowing technically what was needed to insure the success of a production. He was a technician's technician. All well and good there, and his clients and company employees respected him for his knowledge.

But Gerard was *not* a good leader. His style was more command and control instead of investment and modeling. Depending on size and complexity, events often required extended hours and expansive requirements for Gerard and his teams. In that industry this requirement was not abnormal. But Gerard didn't handle leading his people well no matter the size or complexity of the engagement.

While committed to excellent customer service and "making sure it *all* turns out right," Gerard couldn't (or refused to) get a handle on how to motivate his people with anything more than a paycheck. Of course, the paycheck was important—it was the tangible reward for the services of the people who worked hard for him. But this leader never quite understood that people need more than a paycheck.

The failures of Gerard's leadership came from his lack of belief in the positive results his personnel could achieve. Because he didn't make good decisions about the successes of his crews he excessively micromanaged employees, got way too involved in task minutiae, and was often thought to be seen in two places at one time. His crews were convinced he was everywhere at once, directing, working, and interfering.

Joy, one of his newer but highly trusted employees observed this behavioral anomaly time and time again. She noted how Gerard's overbearing presence and overactive demands debilitated the staff, caused confusion and mistrust, and made many employees "just want to be out of his way."

Enough became enough. Joy approached him at one point and deliberately inquired, "Do you want to do my job and everyone else's job, too? Because if that's the case, you're on your own!"

Arrested, Gerard stopped in his tracks. With eyes wide open, he looked at Joy with a new and profound understanding. To his credit, he listened. He learned. In fact, at a subsequent leader's meeting of his top staff (Joy included) he talked about her comments, his actions, and his new choices. He told them he was changing his behavior, and he did.

Belief in positive results always means making decisions about others' success. It also means acting on those decisions. It includes trusting them to do their jobs, equipping them to be successful, training them, correcting errors, and celebrating positive results.

One example: Lincoln took notice of General Ulysses S. Grant, especially as Grant started to win victories in the west. Lincoln also became aware, along with many others that Grant drank a lot. The story goes that some devout clergymen stopped in to see the president, to complain to Lincoln about how much Grant drank, suggesting that Lincoln remove him from command. Lincoln inquired, "What does he drink?" The preachers answered, "Whiskey!" Lincoln probed, "What kind of whiskey?" Apparently they told him. Upon receiving their answer, Lincoln is said to have replied, "Then send a case of this whiskey to *all* my generals! I cannot spare this man: he *fights*."

This story may or may not be true; there are many versions of it. Regardless, it is an interesting anecdote. It *is* true that Lincoln had engaged many generals who had not fought, or who had fought battles and lost most of them. The list of those generals was too long for a commander in chief who knew the stakes of losing a war and a country.

Grant's dogged commitment to winning and the fact that he did win in battle was refreshing to the president. Lincoln needed this general. Grant was one who would share the president's commitment to ending the war by winning it, a necessary measure to reunite the Union. If whiskey was a motivator, then so be it!

Lincoln believed in Grant *and* the cause. It was Lincoln's job to provide Grant what the general needed, to win the war. While that may or may not have included whiskey, Lincoln's belief included his provision. It was not belief alone—it was action based on belief. It was a decision about success that was clearly demonstrated in behavior. Because Lincoln earnestly desired positive results, he made the choice to empower those he led to achieve all they could.

Lesson 14
What Is Cherished Today

"What is cherished today is often composed of what was given up yesterday." (*Lincoln, Leadership and Gettysburg*, page 36)

In an uncertain and insecure world, sacrifice is often required to encourage stabilization, ensure peace, provide resolution to difficult problems, win a war, or rightfully restore property seized by an aggressor. Forms of sacrifice are many. Examples are absence of a loved one, heart-rending loneliness, physical and emotional wounds endured through prolonged suffering, financial duress, and death.

Those in our military who endure such sacrifices are to be honored. Those who serve, regardless of their degrees of sacrifice, are to be thanked, and more than just on Memorial Day or Veteran's Day.

Sacrifice

Sacrifice is the giving up of something held dear on behalf of a greater cause. Many parents understand sacrifice for their children. Warriors understand it when they fight for the country to which they owe their allegiance. What are some of the sacrifices you have seen and with which you are intimately acquainted?

I have lived in San Diego. The Pacific Ocean forms the western border. This city is home to many military installations, including Navy facilities. Few cannot be moved deeply when they observe the exuberance demonstrated by friends and relatives on shore when a naval ship returns from deployment. The joy is nearly overwhelming as warriors disembark their ship and are reunited with their families!

It should be this way. A heartfelt "Welcome Home" conveyed to those who offer up a portion of their lives for the good of the country must never cease.

While degrees of sacrifice vary, one thing does not: the realization that when sacrifice is offered, the end result may be cherished even more because of the costs that were paid. We cherish most what costs us more.

Those who observed the devastation of 911 (September 11, 2001) cannot fail to recall the fire trucks heading *toward* the twin towers in New York City as the people who worked in those buildings rushed *from* them. Millions remember our first responders who hurried into the burning structures as the occupants tried to leave. The photographs are telling as are the stories that continue to be told of the heroism and sacrifice on that horrible day.

And the 911 sacrifices were certainly not limited to Lower Manhattan. Washington D.C., where the Pentagon was hit, and the field near Shanksville, Pennsylvania where United Airlines Flight 93 crashed bear tribute to the memory of those who lost their lives as a result of the cruel attacks of terror. Brave people sought to help those who were hurt and brave people tried to wrest control of a terrorist-commandeered airliner. These people truly are heroes.

What would cause a person to sacrifice to the point of never giving up and perhaps to the point of giving all? Certainly, a belief in a cause and obedience to duty, but perhaps there is more. To many who serve our nation in the ranks of the military, and to those who offer up "the last full measure of devotion" (from Lincoln's Gettysburg Address), the *results* to be achieved must surely outweigh the pain, uncertainty, and even death the cause may demand.

Be Thankful

Let's bring this home. What do you cherish today? Who sacrificed for a cause to ensure the results that you enjoy on the other side of the payment of the costs? Pause and be thankful. Express your appreciation to those who have given so that you can be free. Thank your parents, guardians, grandparents, military personnel, teachers, and other family members and friends for all they have given up for you, to help you achieve as you enjoy the blessings of liberty.

Great teams are composed of thankful people. True thankfulness does not stem from an attitude of entitlement or demand. Heart-felt thankfulness recognizes the value of a gift received and often the value of the giver as well.

Make a list of all the people who have sacrificed for you, and if appreciation doesn't well up from within, check your motives as well as your methods. When any team member makes a decision about another team member's success, that decision *should* cost something and *must* be borne through the actions of the one who gives on behalf of someone else. On the receiving end, the one who benefits from a gift of another best expresses his or her gratitude *by doing the same thing for someone else.*

Cherish is a powerful word. Use it to describe how you treasure not only what you receive from someone else but what you desire to invest in others that they may receive the benefits you enjoy.

It is obvious that giving and receiving are parts of the same action. One cannot exist without the other. When both are engaged, cherishing what was given up yesterday to bring about what we enjoy today is a natural and right reaction.

Glen Aubrey

Excerpt from the Gettysburg Address, Abraham Lincoln, November 19, 1863, Gettysburg, Pennsylvania

This theme was essence of the words of Lincoln's Gettysburg Address, partially quoted above. Here they are in context: "…in a larger sense, we cannot dedicate—we cannot consecrate—we cannot hallow—this ground. The brave men, living and dead, who struggled here, have consecrated it, far above our poor power to add or detract. The world will little note, nor long remember what we say here, but it can never forget what they did here. It is for us the living, rather, to be dedicated here to the unfinished work which they who fought here have thus far so nobly advanced. It is rather for us to be here dedicated to the great task remaining before us—that from these honored dead we take increased devotion to that cause for which they gave *the last full measure of devotion*—that we here highly resolve that these dead shall not have died in vain—that this nation, under God, shall have a new birth of freedom—and that government of the people, by the people, for the people, shall not perish from the earth."

The costs that were paid by those who died framed the *opportunity* and the *obligation* for the ongoing resolutions of those who remain: to assure that the sacrifices given by some would not be unrecognized by any; to assure that those who perished would be remembered forever, and to guarantee that their deeds would continue to be validated within the ongoing fulfillment of duty by those who value the greater cause more than self absorption. It is in the cherishing and the hard work of giving back that a committed and strong individual honors the past, remains faithful in the present, and diligently prepares for better futures for those who will come after.

Lesson 15
Legacies Last Beyond What Is Expedient

When the first version of *Leadership Is—How to Build Your Legacy* was being written in 2004, I had to confront these central truths:

1. Leadership is not inherited—it is chosen.
2. Leadership is not determined by what a leader requires of others—rather, by what that leader gives to others.
3. Leadership is all about investing in others to ensure that a leader's followers are empowered to accomplish more

than the leader may have even thought possible. (See www.LeadershipIs.com.)

There are many models of leadership available from which to choose, and each is a choice. Each model may carry certain traits that are used to distinguish one leadership "style" or "paradigm" from another. Theories abound. Leadership has been relegated to lists of inborn characteristics, so-called laws, titles, positions, and responsibilities. But I believe these models of leadership fall short of what leadership truly is.

Leadership that *lasts* is leadership committed to building legacies that benefit both leaders and followers, now and in the future. Leadership that works well and endures invests, gives itself away, and often is accompanied by costly sacrifices that provide the greatest opportunities for followers to succeed.

This kind of leadership is more about giving than demanding and more about helping than holding onto a position. It's more about promotion of people over production, knowing that when people are treated as more important than what they do, two results are obtained: better people *and* improved output.

Opinions Change, Principles Do Not

Leadership in any organization that rises above providing temporary fixes will meet the needs of today *and* tomorrow because it rests upon enduring principles that do not change instead of endless opinions that frequently do. A variation of these words is found on page 45 of *Lincoln, Leadership and Gettysburg*.

A leadership legacy so constructed survives no matter what comes along and its effects touch everyone it comes in contact with. It is built on bedrock truth that never fluctuates, no matter circumstances, causes, conflicts, or even the characteristics of the personality traits of the person who chooses to lead in this way.

And there is the central point: leadership is a decision about someone else's success that is evidenced in the choice of actions that corroborate the decision. Anyone who decides at any time to make someone else's job more productive and then acts upon that decision is leading.

Opinions change, truths do not. If one wants to lead well and build a legacy that benefits those who come after, that person will base his or her understanding and exercise of leadership on enduring leadership models that have been shown to produce positive rewards no matter the difficulties that must be overcome.

Lincoln did this, again evidenced in his Gettysburg Address. His purpose in composing and delivering the two minute speech encompassed far more than the dedication of a national cemetery, although that intention was certainly part of the assignment he wanted to fulfill. In brief, Lincoln wanted to remind the country of its origin and opportunity as well as its responsibility to honor those who had died and endured sacrifice, to "…secure the blessings of liberty to ourselves and our posterity…" (From the Preamble of the Constitution of the United States)

Freedom

He spoke of "a new birth of freedom" and in that phrase he described what effective and lasting leadership produces: it produces *freedom*. Not bondage, freedom. This is *freedom from* needless restrictions imposed by insecure leaders who are threatened by the success of others and it is *freedom to* opening up the doors of opportunity of unlimited achievement and success.

A great leader is not content with a position obtained. A great leader is content only when his or her followers capture a vision, build on it with the leader's teaching, modeling, encouragement, and support, and create something even better. These meritorious successes become lasting legacies that endure in the lives of those they impact.

Expedient vs. Excellent Leadership

Expedient leadership is all about what may be done today to mitigate a current problem. While not wrong, it's limiting. Excellent leadership looks beyond the expediency of the moment and applies eternal truth to the resolution of issues so that generations to come are benefitted by the choices current leaders make.

If you want to lead well, learn the lessons of enduring leadership and apply them. You will not only solve the problems of today; in the long run you will empower those who have looked to you for leadership to become effective leaders in their own right. These are people who when it is their turn will make the choices destined to produce positive outcomes for succeeding generations. There no greater legacy than this.

Lesson 16
Leaders Learn and Get Involved

In *Lessons of War*, on page 44, we read: "Students of history observe its incidents and issues. They learn from the mistakes and successes of the past. Leaders of today embrace and activate the lessons that have been shown to endure. One of them is this: if a condition is to be improved, leaders act decisively when causes and choices are shown to be right."

Remember that incidents are events and issues are the reasons or causes behind them. From a perspective that includes both, a review of what happened and then why it happened constitutes a balanced approach to handling the incident on one level and dealing with its issue at a deeper one.

True leaders do not lead in a vacuum. We know that effective leadership abhors a leadership vacuum—leaders will fill it every time. This is especially true when history seems to repeat itself and leaders of today have to deal with challenges that are new for *them*. But effective leaders also remember that great leaders of the past faced similar situations. The *exact* history is not duplicated in that names and incidents are different; but the issues *behind* the events demonstrate repeating patterns of human behavior and produce similar results every time.

Leaders Learn from History

For a leader to be the most effective when faced with the tough stuff now, that leader must learn from mistakes and successes of the past (the *what*) and then discover causes behind them (the *why*), *if* that leader truly desires positive outcomes to current problems.

Bottom line: a leader learns and then applies what has been learned. And these efforts never cease.

This "learn from history" requirement not a small study or a casual review for the leader who wants to be the best he or she can be in solving today's negative occurrences, providing positive outcomes. This kind of learning is not a glossing over monumental truth in hopes that something good might come from applying bandages. This learning of history is intentional, focused, and it never stops digging in to discover causes, motives, methods, and eventual results. The goal of this learning is to see the largest picture possible and then descend into the smaller details of principle-based practice so that right solutions can be applied in situations today.

In other words, a leader's understanding of what occurred, who was affected, and in what ways others were impacted forges the opportunity to apply an enduring principle into a current challenge.

Truly effective leaders learn from the past, embrace the principles they learn, and apply them in the present. They know that certain results will likely be achieved when the same principles are practiced in similar situations because human behaviors are not original with the current crop of people with whom a leader deals; behaviors and their motives are embedded in the very fabric of a society in which the leader works and are replicas of abiding principles (good and bad) that have been active since the beginning of human interaction.

It's all about knowing what the principles are that led to the actions that occurred. When positive principles are embraced, positive actions result. When negative principles are embraced, negative actions result. Or, as I used to tell my kids, make good choices and good things happen. Make bad choices, and bad things happen. It's really that simple.

Positive principles are those based on the truth of the dignity of individuals. They promote life and liberty. They incorporate positive values like integrity, compassion, excellence, endurance, and love. Negative principles are their polar opposites, of course. These principles come from believing propositions that are proven to be false, that deny the dignity of people and promote enslavement and destitution. Falsifying information, vengeance, laziness, giving up, and hatred are examples.

Leaders of today embrace and activate the lessons that have been shown to endure, those that create positive undertakings and uplifting results. This means, of course, if you are the leader, you have incredible responsibility along with your authority to assure that your motives are right and true and that your means match your motives. It also means, if you are the follower that you must check your leader's intentions, methods, and results. Does good come from them, or destruction?

Leaders can only promote positive principles when the principles are known, believed, and activated. They do this well when they immerse themselves in truths and actions designed to showcase those positive principles, and work *with* their followers to achieve the results they both want.

Belief and Action

No effective leader lives in principle alone; they *believe* in principle, they talk about it, the embrace it and teach it, but most of all they *act* to affect the changes desired. They turn ideas into deeds and therein resides a central aspect of a successful leader's greatness. It is this: great leadership truly *leads* the way—it doesn't assume an outcome. It *works* for it.

Observe a leader who only *tells* followers what should be done—even if what he or she says promotes right actions—and you will observe a leader who is disconnected from doing and who will eventually fade. It's one thing to teach a person how to swim from poolside, talking about breathing and strokes; it's another to jump into the pool and *demonstrate* how to swim while the instructor works *with* the student to achieve the goal of becoming a swimmer in deeds, not just theory.

A leader is either absent or present when involvement is concerned. The position of *not* being involved eventually results in disconnect and dysfunction. The position of being involved in *real life engagement* is where followers are taught by the leader not only what to do, but how to do it better than the leader ever could. This is effective and enduring leadership at its pinnacle: where a leader's involvement produces results that outlast the leader.

Taking Initiative

Leadership like this begins with taking initiative. *Anyone at anytime who takes the initiative to apply a principle and act upon it to achieve a desired positive result is exercising great leadership.*

Taking initiative can be hard because the one who takes the initiative can be the one who shoulders the greatest risk of failure and the responsibility if an initiative fails. However, that person also invests for the greatest reward and shares the reward if the initiative succeeds.

The one who initiates action is a pace setter. If you are the leader and if you want to lead well, do this: learn from the past then take the initiative to apply positive principles into specific opportunities where uplifting results are desired today.

Again from *Lessons of War*, pages 44 and 45: "Great leaders take the initiative. They change their circumstances for the better. They work diligently to produce positive results for themselves and those they lead. They know that the good they accomplish will forever affect the outcome of a conflict and those who live beyond it."

Never is this truth clearer than when a master instructs an apprentice to accomplish a task at a level that is superior to that of the master. Apart from direct involvement, leaders who want duplicative results will find themselves frustrated at the lack of positive outcomes in the lives or situations of other people. Indeed, their leadership fades when they do.

A superior leader will obtain greater and most positive results through direct involvement birthed in learning, borne on principled action, and committed to a cause beyond casual instruction. These results endure beyond current circumstances and become models of instruction and learning for the new leaders who are coming up.

Lesson 17
Responsibilities Accompany Remembrance and Retelling

History is shared and cannot ever be done over. Remembrance and the retelling of a piece of history bear significant responsibility for a leader who talks about what happened with the intent of teaching the principles of abiding leadership.

A leader who wants to help people and situations improve and achieve enduring positive results for those who follow, never discards history, doesn't try to change it to make situations look better; rather, that leader relates true history and seeks the wisdom within the principles and practices that the history lessons show. From *Lincoln, Leadership and Gettysburg*, pages 58 and 59: "History teaches contemporary and future generations the awesome responsibilities that accompany acts of remembering."

For leaders, remembering an event may be much more than simply treasuring it in the mind. It's all about learning from the memory, too, and sharing what's been learned, good and bad. Everyone treasures memories that bring pleasant emotions. But there is more. If you're the leader and are charged with teaching history, you also must evaluate and communicate occurrences that produced negative outcomes.

Teaching History

When a leader teaches history he or she does so from perspectives of learning *what occurred*, *why* events happened, the *truths* or points inherent in the tales, and *how* these truths can apply in efforts to create solutions for today's challenges.

Telling Stories

Secure leaders often tell stories to their followers to illustrate points they want to make. Often they relate anecdotes that mean the most to them, sometimes using their own foibles as illustrations of what to do and what not to do. The hope is that the "moral" or central meaning of any story will resonate with followers as much as the story itself does.

A leader who relates a story likes it when a follower "gets it" and has his or her own "ah ha" moment—whether producing a solemn reaction or a humorous outburst. A collection of those remembrances and stories are the seeds of great and sometimes momentous lessons where truth has been embedded in real life, and people learn from shared history.

Lincoln was a great storyteller. His storytelling was unique. One thing that made his stories memorable was that they were anchored to real lives of common people and the causes of their day. Read and study hundreds of books on Lincoln's life and pilgrimage and you can't avoid this fact.

Working within towns up and down the judicial circuit in Illinois, from his beginning days as a lawyer, it was not uncommon for the judge, lawyers (from both sides) and other interested parties at the close of a day of judicial proceedings, to adjourn to a nearby watering hole and swap stories until late at night. Lincoln's manner in these early days was one familiar among frontiersmen; he was coarse, blunt, but respectful while cloaking his stories in humorous anecdotes of the day. People loved hearing him.

When he was elected to the highest office of the land, President Lincoln didn't stop telling his stories—in fact he often used them to illustrate momentous truths of the day, to lighten up a situation, or change the direction of a conversation. These stories were born of memories and experiences of common men and women, and they had familiar themes embedded all the way through them.

These tales served the president and his listeners well. In a highly charged and deeply depressing time of war he would often stop in the middle of a cabinet discourse to tell his cabinet members a story or a joke. The fact that he would this was well known. In fact, there were times when he was severely criticized and mocked for telling humorous stories when so many men on both sides of the conflict were dying. At one point Lincoln is known to have said, "If I couldn't tell these stories, I would die." Storytelling helped Lincoln remain sane and grounded and often provided just the release a moment of angst or momentous judgment may have needed.

One story Lincoln is said to have told often was about his homeliness. Most people thought Lincoln was not very good looking. He was tall, angular, coarse, rugged, and uncouth in his mannerisms. His frame was gangly, his hair often uncombed, his clothes didn't fit very well especially in his youth and early career, and he hailed from the "backwoods." All in all, the image most people had of Lincoln was not one of a handsome and cultured man.

One variation of the story he told on himself goes like this: Lincoln was walking alone on a country road one day when a man approached him, stopped him, gazed into his eyes and up and down his face. Presently the man presented Lincoln with a knife, stating, "I want to give this knife to you; this is your personal property." Lincoln responded, "No, I have never owned a knife like this; you must be mistaken." The stranger replied, "No, there is no mistake. The person who gave me this knife said I should give it to anyone I found who was uglier than me, and you sir, certainly fit that description!"

Lincoln's focus in his storytelling was often a truth that the common man would understand. His purpose was to relate to his audience, regardless of size or makeup, some of the history that all of them shared, and his responsibility was to open up opportunities for gems of truth to be uncovered and appreciated—humorous or not.

A responsibility to learn from history means, of course, that we must know our history in order to learn from it. That responsibility embraces uncovering a shared memory and retelling it.

If you're the leader: become well acquainted with the history your group or team should embrace and from which they could learn. Then give them a story now and then to illustrate a truth, embrace a lesson, improve an environment, or change a circumstance. You'll likely be surprised the positive effects assuming that responsibility can produce.

The phrase, "Let me tell you a story..." carries great weight when it attracts the attention of those who would benefit from the telling of a tale, hearing it told, learning its truth, and laughing a little, too, if that's the intent and what is needed. How good a storyteller are you?

Lesson 18
Leaders Recognize Their Limits

Leaders are often put on a pedestal, whether or not they want to be. Many hold the opinion that assuming a position of leadership is akin to living in a fishbowl in that every motive and movement will or should be observed by everyone. To counteract this, many leaders seek solitude when their responsibilities are finished, simply to regain a focus and maintain stability. Sometimes there is no other choice.

If you are the leader you know that there are some activities you choose not to do, some places you dare not go, some conversations from which you should refrain, and some duties that you need not assume. Why? Well, simply because you're the leader does *not* mean that you have the answers to every situation, can give counsel on every circumstance, or have the ability let alone the desire to fix every problem.

Leaders recognize their limits, and they should. Often these limits are self-imposed, and are described as setting and maintaining reasonable boundaries. Some limits are born of people or factors beyond the leader's control. Regardless of source, limits exist. Knowing them is really not optional. When intentionally set by the leader or discovered through courses that life reveals, they are present and must be seen to be what they are: confines that possibly shouldn't be breached, or walls that can't be torn down.

From *Lincoln, Leadership and Gettysburg*, page 68: "Leaders recognize their limits. How they handle what they don't know is as important as how they handle what they do know." And some of the things leaders don't know should likely be left well enough alone unless a leader has to get involved.

There is no abandonment of responsibility when a leader recognizes and honors his or her limits. In fact, that recognition actually defines what a true engagement should be within causes and circumstances that merit and require a leader's involvement.

I remember that many years ago a professional coach and family counselor said to me in a moment of quiet contemplation, "I have come to realize that every problem does not need to be fixed in 55 minutes." He was right!

Leadership carries the responsibility of knowing which situations require the leader's presence and which ones don't. A leader's role includes developing the wisdom to know the difference.

Generally where a leader's involvement invades inappropriately on the turf of others, this invasion could be legitimately construed as micromanaging. Where a leader is not invited his or her voice may not be appreciated or accepted. If a leader's presence or comments violate the confidence of another person (where explicit permission for engagement in any form has not been requested, or if requested has not been granted), that leader should refrain from entering a situation or dealing with the people in it. For leaders who relish solving people's problems (especially if the leader's worth is wrapped up in doing so) these can be tough lessons to learn and follow.

Stages of conflict often reveal opportunities for leaders to honor their limits. Sometimes appropriately limiting involvement is necessary but it may not be easy to do.

Many times in our consulting practice I have stopped short of trying to "fix" a problem *unless* I can receive the right answer to this question (often written): "How strong is your desire for me to solve this and do I have your permission to enter this situation and become involved to the degree that is needed to correct the problem?" The right answer, of course, the one that would permit if not request further in-depth engagement, would be this: "I want your involvement, and yes I give you my permission to help." To further make the point and clarify what may be at stake, I might follow up with another question: "Do I have your permission to quote you and to take this problem to the person or board that may have the authority and responsibility to fix the problem, even if you are shown to be a part of it?"

These can be intimidating questions to some people, especially those who whine about an issue and look less for solutions than they do for a person of authority to agree with them and somehow, they think, validate their position, incorrect or not. Questions like these presented from a pure desire to understand appropriate limits and true possibilities for successful engagement, answered from people with integrity who truly do want help and are willing to be part of a solution (especially if they've been part of the problem), either create open doors of engagement or limits to involvement, and they should.

Leaders who engage must be committed to discovering and implementing solutions. So they had better be sure that the opportunities and necessary agreements exist to proceed before ever entering into what could otherwise be a minefield.

This isn't to say that some issues shouldn't be addressed where a leader decides that he or she must invade a circumstance or issue for the good of a far greater cause or because adherence to law demands it. In fact, though the risks may be higher and they usually are, in these instances the committed leader enters because he or she believes there is *no other choice* than to get directly involved and work for the benefit and the highest good for the welfare of a population.

Such was the case when Lincoln was confronted with the Repeal of the Missouri Compromise in 1854. This was a turning point for the country and for the future president.

Glen Aubrey

Introduction to Lincoln's response on the Repeal of the Missouri Compromise

After Lincoln had finished his first and only term in Congress in 1849, the repeal of the Missouri Compromise "aroused" him again—perhaps to a degree he had never even known before—by his own admission. He had been elected to the U. S. House of Representatives in 1846, but most would conclude that he had remained fairly unknown through his term, though he had introduced resolutions criticizing the president on the entrance of the United States into a war with Mexico. Following his stint in Congress, he had chosen to practice law.

In an autobiographical letter to J. W. Fell, dated December 20, 1859, Lincoln wrote: "I was losing interest in politics when the repeal of the Missouri Compromise aroused me again." Can you imagine how different our country's history might have been were Lincoln *not* to have become interested in politics again?

The repeal of Missouri Compromise may not be a topic that too many people today fully appreciate or understand. It occurred a long time ago. However, the importance of this event cannot be overstated when it comes to illustrating events and circumstances into which leaders *must* inject themselves, those where a cause and higher motive encourage direct involvement rather than abstaining from it.

Introduction to Lincoln's Peoria Speech on the Repeal of the Missouri Compromise

Lincoln gave a speech at Peoria, Illinois on October 16, 1854 in which he addressed the history and his desires regarding the repeal of the Missouri Compromise. The full text of this speech is included at the end of this book. While the speech is long, an earnest reader will note many of the poignant principles and eternal gems of wisdom that Lincoln put forth. That reader will also sense Lincoln's intense desire to proclaim the right and good, and the commitment he showed in telling and living the truths embodied in the Declaration of Independence.

The eager student will note how in the process Lincoln became the spokesperson for a loftier cause he knew was right, based on the founding documents, and how that commitment eventually led him to be elected to the highest office in the land and positioned him to reunite a divided Union torn apart by its civil war.

This Peoria speech was part of an ending to the self-imposed "limit" that Lincoln had adopted for himself, thinking that practicing law would constitute the balance of his career after his role in Congress was concluded. We should be thankful that in this case this "limit" was recognized for what it was, and that Lincoln violated it because something greater was clearly at stake.

The question is never whether leaders should recognize their limits. The question will always be: "How do I understand and deal with my limits as I understand them?" From *Lessons of War*, page 50: "Great leaders choose to accept what they may not know while endeavoring mightily to uphold a greater cause and deal effectively with what they do know."

Lesson 19

A Repeating Cycle of Cause and Effect

The following passage occurs in the 2012 Revised Version of *Leadership Is—How to Build Your Legacy*, pages 56 and 57 under the heading: **The Law of Sowing and Reaping and the Law of Compensation**

Investment leadership initiative derives its being from the models within the Law of Sowing and Reaping and the Law of Compensation. Both are natural laws and high principles. The Law of Sowing and Reaping states that whatever leaders invest into the right soil will be multiplied back in a ratio of many to one. The Law of Compensation says that sure and compensatory reward will follow every action.

Each leader, in consideration of the concepts presented here, views leadership as a venture of elevated importance, one that contains lasting effect, and yields return in duplicative fashion and like manner, exponentially. Leadership's investment carefully considers selections of person, time, place and opportunity and these choices are fulfilled within expanding knowledge (understanding what to do), wisdom (knowing how to do it) and care (anticipating and projecting how what is done will affect others), because results will surely follow.

Emerson has stated, "Every act rewards itself... Cause and effect, means and ends, seed and fruit, cannot be severed; for the effect already blooms in the cause, the end preexists in the means, the fruit in the seed... The nature and soul of things takes on itself the guaranty of the fulfillment of every contract, so that honest service cannot come to loss... Every stroke shall be repaid..."

This model of leadership investment is exclusive and inclusive at the same time. It is exclusive in that it appropriately limits the most transferable investments and greatest vision casting to a narrowed number of followers who have the most opportunity for impact, influence and investment in others with what they have learned; it is inclusive in that the message of core values and people investment, its operational truth-in-action, and the successes of the leader's involvement with the follower are openly presented to a wide audience through the actions of the followers into their networks. People into whom future exclusive investments are made will most likely come out of this wider audience of observers. This cycle of leadership investment becomes a repeating pattern, from leader to follower, and new leader to new follower.

If you are an investor leader, you will own the responsibility to take the initiative to begin a process of life investment into a follower. This process is not casual; rather, it is cause-driven. It is intentional invasion with permission into another person's life and experience." (See www.LeadershipIs.com.)

"What goes around comes around" is a current expression that is commonly used although many of those who use it may not understand how vast its meaning really is. Relate the phrase to leadership and you could conclude that any action by a leader causes a reaction in followers or other leaders. Nothing is done in isolation (that is, without birthing a reaction of some kind) when true leadership is present and active in any environment.

From *Lincoln, Leadership and Gettysburg*, page 70: "Every action bears a reaction; each cause births an effect."

What a leader decides and then chooses to do will impact others, plain and simple. If a leader really wants to make a lasting positive impact, then that leader will seek to understand the principles of sowing and reaping and those of compensation. There really are no alternatives, as the Emerson passage clearly points up.

Communication, Core Principles, and Concrete Action

There are three elements that come together in sowing, reaping, and compensation. When all three are present and active they provide mutual and sustainable support to leaders who act from the knowledge that what they do will last beyond what is done and the circumstances in which they do it. These three elements are *communication*, *core principles*, and *concrete action*.

These three are referenced on page 69 of *Lincoln, Leadership and Gettysburg*. They bear repeating here and this reference requires further explanation.

Great leaders seek to *communicate* well to their followers. Right communication has to do with assuring that what is said is what is heard, and that commensurate action follows a receptivity of truth. As noted earlier, learning becomes living only when behaviors change, so unless behaviors change, hopefully for the better, communication has not fully occurred.

If a leader communicates well, he or she builds a legacy within the reception, understanding, and action of a follower or listener. Where true communication takes place, a reasonable expectation should exist that behaviors will change and resulting action will create a whole new paradigm of opportunity for expanded learning and even more positive change.

Couple right communication with *core principles*. Core principles are the bedrock truths an individual and his or her team adhere to and act upon as they fulfill their tasks. In other words, their actions flow from the identification, acceptance, and obedience to these principles. Principles are communicated through words and deeds where deeds become the demonstrations of the words—the proofs that what was said produced changes in what was done.

It is easy to see that right communication and core principles, if they really mean something, will only be validated in real life through *concrete action* on the part of those who agree. The phrase *concrete action* refers to activities that are done willfully and purposefully to fulfill desires for improvements within needs that must be addressed. And these only happen when behaviors change.

A lasting legacy begins with communication, is emboldened through core principles, and includes behavioral change seen in concrete action. This cycle is repeated in healthy and productive environments. All contribute to and all dwell within the causes and the effects of uplifting leader and follower interactions. This truth simply illustrates once more the correctness of the Emerson quote.

How many times have you as a follower attended team or leadership meetings for your company or workgroup where you considered your presence and perhaps your contributions to be unimportant and the whole event a waste of your time and energy? How many times as a leader have you conducted meetings like that where following the conclusion of the meeting nothing changed?

A meeting without a slate of action steps to be fulfilled is a waste of time. Unless team members understand and agree on their principles and choose to practice what they believe and articulate, that precious resource of time and opportunity just slips away with nothing to show for it. When people know *what* to do and then *do* it because they agree with the principles and requirements of duty, they will ever be part of building a lasting legacy of positive change and beneficial results.

On December 1, 1862 in a message to Congress Lincoln had stated, "We shall nobly save, or meanly lose, the last best hope of earth." Focus on the first two phrases. Even though the words were true, no one in the troubled times of the Civil War could have predicted what a restored Union would mean to the world for generations to come.

What that Congress, Supreme Court, and that President *would do* would reflect what they believed as well as what they said they wanted. It's the same with every administration, legislature, and law interpreting body. In the time frame of the Civil War the decisions and choices those leaders made were momentous, and they knew this. Forward thinking people like Lincoln also recognized the effects of what they accomplished would long outlast their contemporary circumstances, as difficult as they were.

The cause of reuniting the Union would forever alter history. That much was realized—those who made the decisions and choices just couldn't know *how* the final outcomes would unfold. Herein is a central nugget of truth for any leader in troubled or peaceful times: what you do matters. The principles you employ and then demonstrate in your actions will have effects beyond what you know today. Count on it.

"Viewpoints of one generation teach lessons from the past, apply principles in the present, and plan for times yet to come." (*Lincoln, Leadership and Gettysburg*, page 70)

A marked piece of that kind of planning is framing a context into which followers of today contribute as leaders of tomorrow, a part of the never-ending cycle of cause and effect. A leader today must *assure* that to the best of his or her knowledge and ability provision is made so followers who want to succeed can succeed. Patterns established today will be repeated tomorrow. Leaders who want to build lasting legacies must choose models of behavior that can be duplicated and then expanded for even greater positive results for generations to come. They build on the past to forge opportunities for the future.

"Leaders who build legacy recognize their limits and honor the greatness that has preceded them. They consecrate the payments of one generation as they provide a context for current contributions." (*Lincoln, Leadership and Gettysburg*, page 71)

"Teachers and leaders who generate living legacies create opportunities for successors to take their places and accomplish more." (*Lincoln, Leadership and Gettysburg*, page 75)

Welcome to the enduring aspects of superior leadership—its opportunities, responsibilities, struggles, and rewards. Leadership done right is worth it, even if you as the leader are not around to see what you have started.

Lesson 20
Consequences, Good or Bad

Consequences, good and bad, are sure. Like it or not, they come. Their effects may not be fully understood at the time a decision for an action is made by a leader, but generally the more significant the decision and the larger the issue about which a choice is made, the more far-reaching will be its consequences, positive or negative.

History shapes us. We live in the effects of the decisions and choices of our forebears. Note this sentence from *Lincoln, Leadership and Gettysburg*, page 33: "Through declarations, decisions, acts, and consequences, a people—its cultures and world views—are molded and modeled." What may not be as clearly understood because we can't see beyond today is that we are shaping history for generations to come.

To create an improved environment in which those who come after us excel and create their own success stories, leaders of today have to consider the long term aspects of monumental choices. This is true for any leader of any group. It's true for companies, parents and families, institutions of higher education, non-profit organizations, and countries. "Leaders who understand their purpose, place, and responsibility recognize that consequences are not optional. Results always follow actions, good or bad. These leaders prepare for consequences as well as try to fashion them." (*Lincoln, Leadership and Gettysburg*, page 108)

So when it comes to making choices, leaders are drawn, or should be drawn, to the principles that frame their choices. They have to weigh the standards upon which they make their decisions as to quality or detriment of the end results.

What standards do effective leaders choose when they want to construct positive legacies? What are the bedrock principles that have outlasted trial, test, and time, and endure simply because they are right?

I sought to address this very issue in *Leadership Is—How to Build Your Legacy*. The bottom line simply was that the principles that are chosen upon which decisions will be made need to be those that have been *proven* to endure because they are right and true, and because their consequences have been good.

The following passage from *Leadership Is*, beginning on page 171 of the 2012 Revised Version will help to frame our thinking. The context of presentation of enduring principles is what I call a *Value System*, a collection of principled truths, or values, within a system of behavior that has been validated or proven effective over time. Note the term *investment leader* below. The term refers to a leader who wants to invest in others to build a lasting legacy and who runs in an investment track with a follower to accomplish this goal.

A Value System and the Effectiveness Proofs

The formation of a value system where right principles are positioned to produce right practices must be measured against standards that endure. That a list of principled concepts is termed "standards" becomes its own indicator that these attributes of character withstand and have withstood not only tests of time, but the examination of highest qualities that right-standing people embrace. These standards are and have been consistently repeated within lives and works of moral people throughout the millennia whose lives are exemplary.

Whenever these kinds of standards are applied to living, they cause behaviors to change for the better and the quality of life to improve. These standards encourage people of truth to willfully align themselves with what has been shown to work within all natural settings and social environments: culture to culture, continent to continent, and age to age.

A value system in formation must be weighed against standards of proven results. Standards qualify as pillars of character-resilience because they cannot be altered if they are true; none more resilient to human existence will have ever been nor will ever need to be created if the modeled standards are shown to be right and trustworthy. Therefore, a list of standards should not need to be reinvented; indeed, a true list has been around for a very long time.

An investment leader and follower who become engaged in development of a value system as part of their run on the investment leadership track will compare their list of values with a list of solid standards to see if and how their list measures up. The more agreement exists between the enduring standards and their list of core values, the greater the strength of the value system they design and to which they agree to abide.

The list below consists of living standards and these are brought to life and bring life every time they are employed. Indeed they live whether they are employed or not. Your job as the leader is to activate them for you and the people you lead.

These standards constitute nine "proofs" of resiliency and dependability for anyone who wishes to engage in their effectiveness by living out the principled values they produce. They are both tools that can be used to create a value system and the measurement grid of that system's worth. Further, these standards, these indelible proofs, are available to and achievable by anyone at any time. Their use will always alter life. They are "proofs" because, simply put, they've endured in their attestation, and permanently will.

Investment leaders are certain beyond all doubt that to the degree they align themselves and the processes they employ on behalf of their followers to the values that originate with, and produce these proofs, the more unyielding assurances exist that the investments they seek to make will endure for the right reasons, producing results of legacy that will be seen in selfless-serving, other's-benefit ensuing, positive outcomes for as long as they are employed. They reproduce themselves and change every life they touch.

If you are the leader, adapt these, and your legacy will live.

Nine Proofs of a Value System's Validity and Endurance*

1. Love: a decision of the will, evidenced in a commitment and corroborating action to make a positive difference in another's life, regardless of the cost.
2. Joy, or happiness: not necessarily its pursuit, rather, the fulfillment within the processes of seeing and helping another person succeed, where the decisions and engagements that constitute the process are more important than the product and the means because its quality gives birth and credence to its end.
3. Satisfaction, or dwelling in peace: an inner state of involved contentment that originates from acts of doing right things, simply because they are the right things to do, where others are benefited, whether or not they are aware of their benefactors.
4. Patience: a decision to extend forbearance and timely understanding to others and one's self on a journey of personal development that is

often punctuated with pain and problems to overcome.

5. Kindness: deliberate actions toward others that prove to be beneficial to them, caring more about another person's gain than what may or may not come as a reward to the person who generates the good deeds.

6. Goodness: seen or unseen expressions of virtue, morality, and unselfishness, participating in higher standards of ethical activity that elevate others' conditions or places.

7. Faithfulness: the overt evidence of dedication and follow-through seen in consistent obedience to proper authority; where, regardless of circumstances, levels of comfort, perceived or real expectations, or personal cost, a commitment is upheld and fulfilled, period.

8. Gentleness: handling other people's persons, personalities, emotions, welfare, existence and presence with care, consideration, dignity and compassion.

9. Self-control: the desire, decision and cultivated ability to exercise meekness (strength that is utilized by degrees within willful and personally designed confines of correct positioning for greatest and most beneficial results), placing one's self in subjection to lawful order, and the resilience to repeat the behaviors that demonstrate this attribute regardless of time, circumstance, convenience or lack thereof, comfort level, and perceived or real outcomes.

*Ancient Jewish Stoicism literature quoted and adapted by Paul the Apostle (formerly Saul of Tarsus), in Galatians 5:22, 23 of the *Holy Bible* (NIV)

These nine proofs become "The Standards" against which all value systems are measured in terms of origin, application and effectiveness. Where any value system results in all nine proofs in actual experience, that value system can be stated to be "certain" as regards to good character quality, is devoid of inherent defects, and possesses seeds of regenerative longevity in design, nature and projected outcomes, regardless of forms, languages, expressions or means of delivery.

Any value system that does not produce these proofs in whole combination does not constitute a system of meritorious character in its core makeup and should be discarded all together, or reconstructed and realigned to the proofs that stand.

You, as an investor leader, if the investment track is your track of choice, and if you want to build enduring legacy, will see that the constitution of your value system will stand the test of and beyond your time, because it is proven by the standards that have done so. You will remember that the value system erected on these standards uses them as tools for its construction as well as measuring devices of its success, at the same time.

Your job as the leader is to consistently evaluate your behaviors and those of your follower alongside your value system, and your value system next to the nine proofs. You will persevere toward the goal of total concert of relationship and function, demonstrated in whole and in part, and you will encourage your follower to emulate your devotion to this end, because you are building your legacy. Will you do it?

This is an awesome and rewarding responsibility, but one a leader in the investment leadership track welcomes."

From *Lincoln, Leadership and Gettysburg*, page 106: "Dedicated leaders honor and uphold the highest goals for the greatest good." The "greatest good" consists of a higher cause and a more positive outcome, based on enduring principles that have been proven to be beneficial. That "good" becomes the motive (a reason to achieve) and a guide (a beacon of light leaders follow through all kinds of darkness). Both do not waver and the leaders who are committed to accomplishment do not waver, either.

Great leaders set high standards of achievement in setting goals to provide the greatest good. *Honoring* those goals simply means placing them in the forefront of our consideration, letting nothing of lesser value stand in the way of recognizing their importance. *Upholding* these goals means that no matter the trial, test, or tribulation an unwavering leader will commit to their fulfillment regardless of the costs involved, fully aware that great sacrifice may accompany such efforts.

From the same book, page 108: "Leaders who understand their purpose, place, and responsibility recognize that consequences are not optional. Results always follow actions, good or bad. These leaders prepare for consequences as well as try to fashion them." Leaders worth following occupy a unique position in that they help their followers through the challenging times by upholding a model of behavior, and they try to fashion improved outcomes by taking initiative to create better environments where people can excel perhaps beyond what they ever thought possible.

This unique opportunity to help and provide hope fills a leader with responsibility to determine best actions based on best causes, then to take the initiatives to lead others toward the fulfillment of agreed goals. Think about it: "Leadership submits when it recognizes that needs for improvements exist. Leadership perseveres when it determines a course of action is right." (*Lincoln, Leadership and Gettysburg*, page 94)

If a leader doesn't submit to a higher cause and the understanding that in order to improve a situation he or she must get involved, then there will be no determination of a course of action that would require perseverance to complete. A leader practices submission when he or she is shown a need or discovers an opportunity to fashion a better future.

Leaders and their followers who understand that their actions will produce consequences, good or bad, have to cooperate on the basis of their agreement to achieve the results they want. Apart from this cooperation there would be chaos. Chaos happens when team members try to build upon what they don't agree. It doesn't work. In business, we see it far too often as communication breaks down or is non-existent, or as core team principles are thrown to the wind because of a lack of commitment to uphold them, or as concrete action simply doesn't happen because of ignorance, fear, inability, incompetence, ignorance, or just plain laziness.

From *Lessons of War*, page 110: "The directive is this: build upon what you agree, not upon what you do not agree." Teams and their leaders who follow that advice stand a much better chance of success now and of positive legacy outcomes later. Good consequences are almost always assured when a team cooperates on a goal founded upon enduring right principles upon which full agreement exists. Commitments to fulfillment are integral parts of the decisions and choices they make.

No one knows the future, although many try to predict it. Faith systems throughout the world prognosticate the end of time, the doom of man, or the return of Christ, to name a few. Clearly the intent in this book is not to deal in prophecy. The intent here is to affirm the fact that *we simply don't know what we don't know*. Accept it. Believe what you want and be assured in your faith, but also be assured that the future hasn't happened yet, so be extremely careful about predicting any outcomes.

What we *can* be assured of, however, is that the future is coming; it's in fact already here. By the time you read this your moment in the present is past.

A focus on the future *has* to include the fact that even though we may not be able to predict accurately what *will* happen tomorrow or the next day, we *can* fashion frameworks of success that no matter what happens in future months or years leaders and their followers *can* function well based on right principle as they *uphold* worthy causes proven to be true.

For leaders and their followers who want to fashion best outcomes, "…try to obtain all available facts before rendering a decision whose choice will affect not only outcomes, but the lives of people who must live within its results. Understand that only upon the basis of complete facts can an accurate decision and choice be made. Also understand that you may have to make a decision even when all the facts are not known and any choice you make will affect others who must live within the consequences of your choice. In these circumstances a great leader looks to God for higher and more complete wisdom." (*Lessons of War*, page 96)

A mixture of facts and faith exists in any leadership paradigm when consequences of actions are considered. And they have to be considered. Purposed endeavor and final judgment as to success or failure of an endeavor will become pieces of history as early as two seconds from now.

The longer history develops the more clarity as to cause and effect is revealed. But where it can be shown that a leader and his or her team diligently endeavors to base decisions and choices upon enduring principles, proclaim and fight for righteous (upright) causes, and to uphold the greater good, the more it will likely be determined, as a part of *their* history, that they accomplished what they set out to do and improved a situation, creating positive results and an enduring legacy. Also the more likely it is that history will show they submitted to Higher Authority and left final judgments up to God. It will be shown they fulfilled their duties well because they were the ones who decided on the right and did the right because they were convinced through indelible proofs over time that their actions were right and therefore would produce meritorious results.

From *Lessons of War*, page 84: "If you are the leader, embrace these principles:

1. Remain focused on your righteous purpose. (*Righteous* is defined here as *right standing*).
2. Complete your tasks to the best of your ability.
3. In your desires for justice, place final results and judgments of men and means in the hands of God, that all shall be accomplished in accordance to His will."

Ask yourself: "What kinds of consequences do I want to produce: good or bad ones?" It's a simple question with momentous meaning. Here's another: "What kind of legacy do I want to create for those who follow me?" Your actions will produce the consequences of your design and your legacy will be formed in the process. You are in charge of the choices you make in this regard.

Choose your actions now based on the principles you are convinced are true. These choices will go a long way to providing a future that others will be grateful for, in which they also will learn from your model how to design an even greater outcome than perhaps you ever considered.

Speech on the Repeal of the Missouri Compromise

Abraham Lincoln

October 16, 1854

Peoria, Illinois

The repeal of the Missouri Compromise, and the propriety of its restoration, constitute the subject of what I am about to say.

As I desire to present my own connected view of this subject, my remarks will not be, specifically, an answer to Judge Douglas; yet, as I proceed, the main points he has presented will arise, and will receive such respectful attention as I may be able to give them.

I wish further to say, that I do not propose to question the patriotism, or to assail the motives of any man, or class of men; but rather to strictly confine myself to the naked merits of the question.

I also wish to be no less than National in all the positions I may take; and whenever I take ground which others have thought, or may think, narrow, sectional and dangerous to the Union, I hope to give a reason, which will appear sufficient, at least to some, why I think differently.

And, as this subject is no other, than part and parcel of the larger general question of domestic-slavery, I wish to MAKE and to KEEP the distinction between the EXISTING institution, and the EXTENSION of it, so broad, and so clear, that no honest man can misunderstand me, and no dishonest one, successfully misrepresent me.

In order to [get?] a clear understanding of what the Missouri Compromise is, a short history of the preceding kindred subjects will perhaps be proper. When we established our independence, we did not own, or claim, the country to which this compromise applies. Indeed, strictly speaking, the confederacy then owned no country at all; the States respectively owned the country within their limits; and some of them owned territory beyond their strict State limits. Virginia thus owned the North-Western territory—the country out of which the principal part of Ohio, all Indiana, all Illinois, all Michigan and all Wisconsin, have since been formed. She also owned (perhaps within her then limits) what has since been formed into the State of Kentucky. North Carolina thus owned what is now the State of Tennessee; and South Carolina and Georgia, in separate parts, owned what are now Mississippi and Alabama. Connecticut, I think, owned the little remaining part of Ohio—being the same where they now send Giddings to Congress, and beat all creation at making cheese. These territories, together with the States themselves, constituted all the country over which the confederacy then claimed any sort of jurisdiction. We were then living under the Articles of Confederation, which were superceded [*sic*] by the Constitution several years afterwards. The question of ceding these territories to the general government was set on foot.

Mr. Jefferson, the author of the Declaration of Independence, and otherwise a chief actor in the revolution; then a delegate in Congress; afterwards twice President; who was, is, and perhaps will continue to be, the most distinguished politician of our history; a Virginian by birth and continued residence, and withal, a slave-holder; conceived the idea of taking that occasion, to prevent slavery ever going into the north-western territory. He prevailed on the Virginia Legislature to adopt his views, and to cede the territory, making the prohibition of slavery therein, a condition of the deed. Congress accepted the cession, with the condition; and in the first Ordinance (which the acts of Congress were then called) for the government of the territory, provided that slavery should never be permitted therein. This is the famed ordinance of '87 so often spoken of. Thenceforward, for sixty-one years, and until in 1848, the last scrap of this territory came into the Union as the State of Wisconsin, all parties acted in quiet obedience to this ordinance. It is now what Jefferson foresaw and intended—the happy home of teeming millions of free, white, prosperous people, and no slave amongst them.

Thus, with the author of the Declaration of Independence, the policy of prohibiting slavery in new territory originated. Thus, away back of the constitution, in the pure fresh, free breath of the revolution, the State of Virginia, and the National congress put that policy in practice. Thus through sixty odd of the best years of the republic did that policy steadily work to its great and beneficent end. And thus, in those five states, and five millions of free, enterprising people, we have before us the rich fruits of this policy

But now new light breaks upon us. Now congress declares this ought never to have been; and the like of it, must never be again. The sacred right of self-government is grossly violated by it! We even find some men, who drew their first breath, and every other breath of their lives, under this very restriction, now live in dread of absolute suffocation, if they should be restricted in the "sacred right" of taking slaves to Nebraska. That perfect liberty they sigh for—the liberty of making slaves of other people—Jefferson never thought of; their own father never thought of; they never thought of themselves, a year ago. How fortunate for them, they did not sooner become sensible of their great misery! Oh, how difficult it is to treat with respect, such assaults upon all we have ever really held sacred.

Abraham Lincoln—Speech on the Repeal of the Missouri Compromise

But to return to history. In 1803 we purchased what was then called Louisiana, of France. It included the now states of Louisiana, Arkansas, Missouri, and Iowa; also the territory of Minnesota, and the present bone of contention, Kansas and Nebraska. Slavery already existed among the French at New Orleans; and, to some extent, at St. Louis. In 1812 Louisiana came into the Union as a slave state, without controversy. In 1818 or '19, Missouri showed signs of a wish to come in with slavery. This was resisted by northern members of Congress; and thus began the first great slavery agitation in the nation. This controversy lasted several months, and became very angry and exciting; the House of Representatives voting steadily for the prohibition of slavery in Missouri, and the Senate voting as steadily against it. Threats of breaking up the Union were freely made; and the ablest public men of the day became seriously alarmed. At length a compromise was made, in which, like all compromises, both sides yielded something. It was a law passed on the 6th day of March, 1820, providing that Missouri might come into the Union with slavery, but that in all the remaining part of the territory purchased of France, which lies north of 36 degrees and 30 minutes north latitude, slavery should never be permitted. This provision of law, is the Missouri Compromise. In excluding slavery North of the line, the same language is employed as in the Ordinance of '87. It directly applied to Iowa, Minnesota, and to the present bone of contention, Kansas and Nebraska. Whether there should or should not, be slavery south of that line, nothing was said in the law; but Arkansas constituted the principal remaining part, south of the line; and it has since been admitted as a slave state without serious controversy. More recently, Iowa, north of the line, came in as a free state without controversy. Still later, Minnesota, north of the line, had a territorial organization without controversy. Texas principally south of the line, and West of Arkansas; though originally within the purchase from France, had, in 1819, been traded off to Spain, in our treaty for the acquisition of Florida. It had thus become a part of Mexico. Mexico revolutionized and became independent of Spain. American citizens began settling rapidly, with their slaves in the southern part of Texas. Soon they revolutionized against Mexico, and established an independent government of their own, adopting a constitution, with slavery, strongly resembling the constitutions of our slave states. By still another rapid move, Texas, claiming a boundary much further West, than when we parted with her in 1819, was brought back to the United States, and admitted into the Union as a slave state. There then was little or no settlement in the northern part of Texas, a considerable portion of which lay north of the Missouri line; and in the resolutions admitting her into the Union, the Missouri restriction was expressly extended westward across her territory. This was in 1845, only nine years ago.

Thus originated the Missouri Compromise; and thus has it been respected down to 1845. And even four years later, in 1849, our distinguished Senator, in a public address, held the following language in relation to it: "The Missouri Compromise had been in practical operation for about a quarter of a century, and had received the sanction and approbation of men of all parties in every section of the Union. It had allayed all sectional jealousies and irritations growing out of this vexed question, and harmonized and tranquilized the whole country. It had given to Henry Clay, as its prominent champion, the proud sobriquet of the "Great Pacificator " and by that title and for that service, his political friends had repeatedly appealed to the people to rally under his standard, as a presidential candidate, as the man who had exhibited the patriotism and the power to suppress, an unholy and treasonable agitation, and preserve the Union. He was not aware that any man or any party from any section of the Union, had ever urged as an objection to Mr. Clay, that he was the great champion of the Missouri Compromise. On the contrary, the effort was made by the opponents of Mr. Clay, to prove that he was not entitled to the exclusive merit of that great patriotic measure, and that the honor was equally due to others as well as to him, for securing its adoption—that it had its origin in the hearts of all patriotic men, who desired to preserve and perpetuate the blessings of our glorious Union—an origin akin that of the constitution of the United States, conceived in the same spirit of fraternal affection, and calculated to remove forever, the only danger, which seemed to threaten, at some distant day, to sever the social bond of union. All the evidences of public opinion at that day, seemed to indicate that this Compromise had been canonized in the hearts of the American people, as a sacred thing which no ruthless hand would ever be reckless enough to disturb." I do not read this extract to involve Judge Douglas in an inconsistency. If he afterwards thought he had been wrong, it was right for him to change. I bring this forward merely to show the high estimate placed on the Missouri Compromise by all parties up to so late as the year 1849.

But, going back a little, in point of time, our war with Mexico broke out in 1846. When Congress was about adjourning that session, President Polk asked them to place two millions of dollars under his control, to be used by him in the recess, if found practicable and expedient, in negotiating a treaty of peace with Mexico, and acquiring some part of her territory. A bill was duly got up, for the purpose, and was progressing swimmingly, in the House of Representatives, when a member by the name of David Wilmot, a democrat from Pennsylvania, moved as an amendment "Provided that in any territory thus acquired, there shall never be slavery."

This is the origin of the far-famed "Wilmot Proviso." It created a great flutter; but it stuck like wax, was voted into the bill, and the bill passed with it through the House. The Senate, however, adjourned without final action on it and so both appropriation and proviso were lost, for the time. The war continued, and at the next session, the president renewed his request for the appropriation, enlarging the amount, I think, to three million. Again came the proviso; and defeated the measure. Congress adjourned again, and the war went on. In Dec. 1847, the new congress assembled. I was in the lower House that term. The "Wilmot Proviso" or the principle of it, was constantly coming up in some shape or other, and I think I may venture to say I voted for it at least forty times; during the short term I was there. The Senate, however, held it in check, and it never became law. In the spring of 1848 a treaty of peace was made with Mexico; by which we obtained that portion of her country which now constitutes the territories of New Mexico and Utah, and the now state of California. By this treaty the Wilmot Proviso was defeated, as so far as it was intended to be, a condition of the acquisition of territory. Its friends however, were still determined to find some way to restrain slavery from getting into the new country. This new acquisition lay directly West of our old purchase from France, and extended west to the Pacific ocean—and was so situated that if the Missouri line should be extended straight West, the new country would be divided by such extended line, leaving some North and some South of it. On Judge Douglas' motion a bill, or provision of a bill, passed the Senate to so extend the Missouri line. The Proviso men in the House, including myself, voted it down, because by implication, it gave up the Southern part to slavery, while we were bent on having it all free.

In the fall of 1848 the gold mines were discovered in California. This attracted people to it with unprecedented rapidity, so that on, or soon after, the meeting of the new congress in Dec., 1849, she already had a population of nearly a hundred thousand, had called a convention, formed a state constitution, excluding slavery, and was knocking for admission into the Union. The Proviso men, of course were for letting her in, but the Senate, always true to the other side would not consent to her admission. And there California stood, kept out of the Union, because she would not let slavery into her borders. Under all the circumstances perhaps this was not wrong. There were other points of dispute, connected with the general question of slavery, which equally needed adjustment. The South clamored for a more efficient fugitive slave law. The North clamored for the abolition of a peculiar species of slave trade in the District of Columbia, in connection with which, in view from the windows of the capitol, a sort of negro-livery stable, where droves of negroes were collected, temporarily kept, and finally taken to Southern markets, precisely like droves of horses, had been openly maintained for fifty years. Utah and New Mexico needed territorial governments; and whether slavery should or should not be prohibited within them, was another question. The indefinite Western boundary of Texas was to be settled. She was received a slave state; and consequently the farther West the slavery men could push her boundary, the more slave country they secured. And the farther East the slavery opponents could thrust the boundary back, the less slave ground was secured. Thus this was just as clearly a slavery question as any of the others.

These points all needed adjustment; and they were all held up, perhaps wisely to make them help to adjust one another. The Union, now, as in 1820, was thought to be in danger; and devotion to the Union rightfully inclined men to yield somewhat, in points where nothing else could have so inclined them. A compromise was finally effected. The south got their new fugitive-slave law; and the North got California, (the far best part of our acquisition from Mexico,) as a free State. The south got a provision that New Mexico and Utah, when admitted as States, may come in with or without slavery as they may then choose; and the north got the slave-trade abolished in the District of Columbia. The north got the western boundary of Texas, thence further back eastward than the south desired; but, in turn, they gave Texas ten millions of dollars, with which to pay her old debts. This is the Compromise of 1850.

Preceding the Presidential election of 1852, each of the great political parties, democrats and whigs, met in convention, and adopted resolutions endorsing the compromise of '50; as a "finality," a final settlement, so far as these parties could make it so, of all slavery agitation. Previous to this, in 1851, the Illinois Legislature had indorsed it.

During this long period of time Nebraska had remained, substantially an uninhabited country, but now emigration to, and settlement within it began to take place. It is about one third as large as the present United States, and its importance so long overlooked, begins to come into view. The restriction of slavery by the Missouri Compromise directly applies to it; in fact, was first made, and has since been maintained, expressly for it. In 1853, a bill to give it a territorial government passed the House of Representatives, and, in the hands of Judge Douglas, failed of passing the Senate only for want of time. This bill contained no repeal of the Missouri Compromise. Indeed, when it was assailed because it did not contain such repeal, Judge Douglas defended it in its existing form. On January 4th, 1854, Judge Douglas introduces a new bill to give Nebraska territorial government. He accompanies this bill with a report, in which last, he expressly recommends that the Missouri Compromise shall neither be affirmed nor repealed.

Before long the bill is so modified as to make two territories instead of one; calling the Southern one Kansas. Also, about a month after the introduction of the bill, on the judge's own motion, it is so amended as to declare the Missouri Compromise inoperative and void; and, substantially, that the People who go and settle there may establish slavery, or exclude it, as they may see fit. In this shape the bill passed both branches of congress, and became a law.

This is the repeal of the Missouri Compromise. The foregoing history may not be precisely accurate in every particular; but I am sure it is sufficiently so, for all the uses I shall attempt to make of it, and in it, we have before us, the chief material enabling us to correctly judge whether the repeal of the Missouri Compromise is right or wrong.

I think, and shall try to show, that it is wrong; wrong in its direct effect, letting slavery into Kansas and Nebraska—and wrong in its prospective principle, allowing it to spread to every other part of the wide world, where men can be found inclined to take it.

This declared indifference, but as I must think, covert real zeal for the spread of slavery, I cannot but hate. I hate it because of the monstrous injustice of slavery itself. I hate it because it deprives our republican example of its just influence in the world—enables the enemies of free institutions, with plausibility, to taunt us as hypocrites—causes the real friends of freedom to doubt our sincerity, and especially because it forces so many really good men amongst ourselves into an open war with the very fundamental principles of civil liberty—criticizing the Declaration of Independence, and insisting that there is no right principle of action but self-interest.

Before proceeding, let me say I think I have no prejudice against the Southern people. They are just what we would be in their situation. If slavery did not now exist amongst them, they would not introduce it. If it did now exist amongst us, we should not instantly give it up. This I believe of the masses north and south. Doubtless there are individuals, on both sides, who would not hold slaves under any circumstances; and others who would gladly introduce slavery anew, if it were out of existence. We know that some southern men do free their slaves, go north, and become tip-top abolitionists; while some northern ones go south, and become most cruel slave-masters.

When southern people tell us they are no more responsible for the origin of slavery, than we; I acknowledge the fact. When it is said that the institution exists; and that it is very difficult to get rid of it, in any satisfactory way, I can understand and appreciate the saying. I surely will not blame them for not doing what I should not know how to do myself. If all earthly power were given me, I should not know what to do, as to the existing institution. My first impulse would be to free all the slaves, and send them to Liberia,—to their own native land. But a moment's reflection would convince me, that whatever of high hope, (as I think there is) there may be in this, in the long run, its sudden execution is impossible. If they were all landed there in a day, they would all perish in the next ten days; and there are not surplus shipping and surplus money enough in the world to carry them there in many times ten days. What then? Free them all, and keep them among us as underlings? Is it quite certain that this betters their condition? I think I would not hold one in slavery, at any rate; yet the point is not clear enough for me to denounce people upon. What next? Free them, and make them politically and socially, our equals? My own feelings will not admit of this; and if mine would, we well know that those of the great mass of white people will not. Whether this feeling accords with justice and sound judgment, is not the sole question, if indeed, it is any part of it. A universal feeling, whether well or ill-founded, can not [*sic*] be safely disregarded. We can not [*sic*], then, make them equals. It does seem to me that systems of gradual emancipation might be adopted; but for their tardiness in this, I will not undertake to judge our brethren of the south.

When they remind us of their constitutional rights, I acknowledge them, not grudgingly, but fully, and fairly; and I would give them any legislation for the reclaiming of their fugitives, which should not, in its stringency, be more likely to carry a free man into slavery, than our ordinary criminal laws are to hang an innocent one.

But all this; to my judgment, furnishes no more excuse for permitting slavery to go into our own free territory, than it would for reviving the African slave trade by law. The law which forbids the bringing of slaves from Africa; and that which has so long forbid the taking them to Nebraska, can hardly be distinguished on any moral principle; and the repeal of the former could find quite as plausible excuses as that of the latter.

The arguments by which the repeal of the Missouri Compromise is sought to be justified, are these: First, that the Nebraska country needed a territorial government. Second, that in various ways, the public had repudiated it, and demanded the repeal; and therefore should not now complain of it.

And lastly, that the repeal establishes a principle, which is intrinsically right.

I will attempt an answer to each of them in its turn.

First, then, if that country was in need of a territorial organization, could it not have had it as well without as with the repeal? Iowa and Minnesota, to both of which the Missouri restriction applied, had, without its repeal, each in succession, territorial organizations. And even, the year before, a bill for Nebraska itself, was within an ace of passing, without the repealing clause; and this in the hands of the same men who are now the champions of repeal. Why no necessity then for the repeal? But still later, when this very bill was first brought in, it contained no repeal. But, say they, because the public had demanded, or rather commanded the repeal, the repeal was to accompany the organization, whenever that should occur.

Now I deny that the public ever demanded any such thing—ever repudiated the Missouri Compromise—ever commanded its repeal. I deny it, and call for the proof. It is not contended, I believe, that any such command has ever been given in express terms. It is only said that it was done in principle. The support of the Wilmot Proviso, is the first fact mentioned, to prove that

Abraham Lincoln—Speech on the Repeal of the Missouri Compromise

the Missouri restriction was repudiated in principle, and the second is, the refusal to extend the Missouri line over the country acquired from Mexico. These are near enough alike to be treated together. The one was to exclude the chances of slavery from the whole new acquisition by the lump; and the other was to reject a division of it, by which one half was to be given up to those chances. Now whether this was a repudiation of the Missouri line, in principle, depends upon whether the Missouri law contained any principle requiring the line to be extended over the country acquired from Mexico. I contend it did not. I insist that it contained no general principle, but that it was, in every sense, specific. That its terms limit it to the country purchased from France, is undenied [*sic*] and undeniable. It could have no principle beyond the intention of those who made it. They did not intend to extend the line to country which they did not own. If they intended to extend it, in the event of acquiring additional territory, why did they not say so? It was just as easy to say, that "in all the country west of the Mississippi, which we now own, or may hereafter acquire there shall never be slavery," as to say, what they did say; and they would have said it if they had meant it. An intention to extend the law is not only not mentioned in the law, but is not mentioned in any contemporaneous history. Both the law itself, and the history of the times are a blank as to any principle of extension; and by neither the known rules for construing statutes and contracts, nor by common sense, can any such principle be inferred.

Another fact showing the specific character of the Missouri law—showing that it intended no more than it expressed—showing that the line was not intended as a universal dividing line between free and slave territory, present and prospective—north of which slavery could never go—is the fact that by that very law, Missouri came in as a slave state, north of the line. If that law contained any prospective principle, the whole law must be looked to in order to ascertain what the principle was. And by this rule, the south could fairly contend that inasmuch as they got one slave state north of the line at the inception of the law, they have the right to have another given them north of it occasionally—now and then in the indefinite westward extension of the line. This demonstrates the absurdity of attempting to deduce a prospective principle from the Missouri Compromise line.

When we voted for the Wilmot Proviso, we were voting to keep slavery out of the whole Missouri [Mexican?] acquisition; and little did we think we were thereby voting, to let it into

Abraham Lincoln—Speech on the Repeal of the Missouri Compromise

Nebraska, laying several hundred miles distant. When we voted against extending the Missouri line, little did we think we were voting to destroy the old line, then of near thirty years standing. To argue that we thus repudiated the Missouri Compromise is no less absurd than it would be to argue that because we have, so far, forborne to acquire Cuba, we have thereby, in principle, repudiated our former acquisitions, and determined to throw them out of the Union! No less absurd than it would be to say that because I may have refused to build an addition to my house, I thereby have decided to destroy the existing house! And if I catch you setting fire to my house, you will turn upon me and say I INSTRUCTED you to do it! The most conclusive argument, however, that, while voting for the Wilmot Proviso, and while voting against the EXTENSION of the Missouri line, we never thought of disturbing the original Missouri Compromise, is found in the facts, that there was then, and still is, an unorganized tract of fine country, nearly as large as the state of Missouri, lying immediately west of Arkansas, and south of the Missouri Compromise line; and that we never attempted to prohibit slavery as to it. I wish particular attention to this. It adjoins the original Missouri Compromise line, by its northern boundary; and consequently is part of the country, into which, by implication, slavery was permitted to go, by that compromise. There it has lain open ever since, and there it still lies. And yet no effort has been made at any time to wrest it from the south. In all our struggles to prohibit slavery within our Mexican acquisitions, we never so much as lifted a finger to prohibit it, as to this tract. Is not this entirely conclusive that at all times, we have held the Missouri Compromise as a sacred thing; even when against ourselves, as well as when for us?

Senator Douglas sometimes says the Missouri line itself was, in principle, only an extension of the line of the ordinance of '87—that is to say, an extension of the Ohio river. I think this is weak enough on its face. I will remark, however that, as a glance at the map will show, the Missouri line is a long way farther South than the Ohio; and that if our Senator, in proposing his extension, had stuck to the principle of jogging southward, perhaps it might not have been voted down so readily.

But next it is said that the compromises of '50 and the ratification of them by both political parties, in '52, established a new principle, which required the repeal of the Missouri Compromise. This again I deny. I deny it, and demand the proof. I have already stated fully what the compromises of '50 are. The particular part of those measures, for which the virtual repeal of the Missouri compromise is sought to be inferred (for it is admitted they contain nothing about it, in express terms) is the provision in the Utah and New Mexico laws, which permits them when they seek admission into the Union as States, to come in with or without slavery as they shall then see fit. Now I insist this provision was made for Utah and New Mexico, and for no other place whatever. It had no more direct reference to Nebraska than it had to the territories of the moon. But, say they, it had reference to Nebraska, in principle. Let us see. The North consented to this provision, not because they considered it right in itself; but because they were compensated—paid for it. They, at the same time, got California into the Union as a free State. This was far the best part of all they had struggled for by the Wilmot Proviso.

They also got the area of slavery somewhat narrowed in the settlement of the boundary of Texas. Also, they got the slave trade abolished in the District of Columbia. For all these desirable objects the North could afford to yield something; and they did yield to the South the Utah and New Mexico provision. I do not mean that the whole North, or even a majority, yielded, when the law passed; but enough yielded, when added to the vote of the South, to carry the measure. Now can it be pretended that the principle of this arrangement requires us to permit the same provision to be applied to Nebraska, without any equivalent at all? Give us another free State; press the boundary of Texas still further back, give us another step toward the destruction of slavery in the District, and you present us a similar case. But ask us not to repeat, for nothing, what you paid for in the first instance. If you wish the thing again, pay again. That is the principle of the compromises of '50, if indeed they had any principles beyond their specific terms—it was the system of equivalents.

Again, if Congress, at that time, intended that all future territories should, when admitted as States, come in with or without slavery, at their own option, why did it not say so? With such an [sic] universal provision, all know the bills could not have passed. Did they, then—could they—establish a principle contrary to their own intention? Still further, if they intended to establish the principle that wherever Congress had control, it should be left to the people to do as they thought fit with slavery why did they not authorize the people of the District of Columbia at their adoption to abolish slavery within these limits? I personally know that this has not been left undone, because it was unthought [sic] of. It was frequently spoken of by members of Congress and by citizens of Washington six years ago; and I heard no one express a doubt that a system of gradual emancipation, with compensation to owners, would meet the approbation of a large majority of the white people of the District. But without the action of Congress they could say nothing; and Congress said "no." In the measures of 1850 Congress had the subject of slavery in the District expressly in hand. If they were then establishing the principle of allowing the people to do as they please with slavery, why did they not apply the principle to that people?

Again, it is claimed that by the Resolutions of the Illinois Legislature, passed in 1851, the repeal of the Missouri compromise was demanded. This I deny also. Whatever may be worked out by a criticism of the language of those resolutions, the people have never understood them as being any more than an endorsement of the compromises of 1850; and a release of our Senators from voting for the Wilmot Proviso. The whole people are living witnesses, that this only, was their view. Finally, it is asked "If we did not mean to apply the Utah and New Mexico provision, to all future territories, what did we mean, when we, in 1852, endorsed the compromises of '50?"

For myself, I can answer this question most easily. I meant not to ask a repeal, or modification of the fugitive slave law. I meant not to ask for the abolition of slavery in the District of Columbia. I meant not to resist the admission of Utah and New Mexico, even should they ask to come in as slave States. I meant nothing about additional territories, because, as I understood, we then had no territory whose character as to slavery was not already settled. As to Nebraska, I regarded its character as being fixed, by the Missouri compromise, for thirty years—as unalterably fixed as that of my own home in Illinois. As to new acquisitions I said "sufficient unto the day is the evil thereof." When we make new acquaintances, [acquisitions?] we will, as heretofore, try to manage them somehow. That is my answer. That is what I meant and said; and I appeal to the people to say, each for himself, whether that was not also the universal meaning of the free States.

And now, in turn, let me ask a few questions. If by any, or all these matters, the repeal of the Missouri Compromise was commanded, why was not the command sooner obeyed? Why was the repeal omitted in the Nebraska bill of 1853? Why was it omitted in the original bill of 1854? Why, in the accompanying report, was such a repeal characterized as a departure from the course pursued in 1850? and its continued omission recommended?

Abraham Lincoln—Speech on the Repeal of the Missouri Compromise

I am aware Judge Douglas now argues that the subsequent express repeal is no substantial alteration of the bill. This argument seems wonderful to me. It is as if one should argue that white and black are not different. He admits, however, that there is a literal change in the bill; and that he made the change in deference to other Senators, who would not support the bill without. This proves that those other Senators thought the change a substantial one; and that the Judge thought their opinions worth deferring to. His own opinions, therefore, seem not to rest on a very firm basis even in his own mind—and I suppose the world believes, and will continue to believe, that precisely on the substance of that change this whole agitation has arisen.

I conclude then, that the public never demanded the repeal of the Missouri compromise.

I now come to consider whether the repeal, with its avowed principle, is intrinsically right. I insist that it is not. Take the particular case. A controversy had arisen between the advocates and opponents of slavery, in relation to its establishment within the country we had purchased of France. The southern, and then best part of the purchase, was already in as a slave state. The controversy was settled by also letting Missouri in as a slave

State; but with the agreement that within all the remaining part of the purchase, North of a certain line, there should never be slavery. As to what was to be done with the remaining part south of the line, nothing was said; but perhaps the fair implication was, that it should come in with slavery if it should so choose. The southern part, except a portion heretofore mentioned, afterwards did come in with slavery, as the State of Arkansas. All these many years since 1820, the Northern part had remained a wilderness. At length settlements began in it also. In due course, Iowa, came in as a free State, and Minnesota was given a territorial government, without removing the slavery restriction. Finally the sole remaining part, North of the line, Kansas and Nebraska, was to be organized; and it is proposed, and carried, to blot out the old dividing line of thirty-four years standing, and to open the whole of that country to the introduction of slavery. Now, this, to my mind, is manifestly unjust. After an angry and dangerous controversy, the parties made friends by dividing the bone of contention. The one party first appropriates her own share, beyond all power to be disturbed in the possession of it; and then seizes the share of the other party. It is as if two starving men had divided their only loaf; the one had hastily swallowed his half, and then grabbed the other half just as he was putting it to his mouth!

Abraham Lincoln—Speech on the Repeal of the Missouri Compromise

Let me here drop the main argument, to notice what I consider rather an inferior matter. It is argued that slavery will not go to Kansas and Nebraska, in any event. This is a palliation—a lullaby. I have some hope that it will not; but let us not be too confident. As to climate, a glance at the map shows that there are five slave States—Delaware, Maryland, Virginia, Kentucky, and Missouri—and also the District of Columbia, all north of the Missouri compromise line. The census returns of 1850 show that, within these, there are 867,276 slaves—being more than one-fourth of all the slaves in the nation.

It is not climate, then, that will keep slavery out of these territories. Is there anything in the peculiar nature of the country? Missouri adjoins these territories, by her entire western boundary, and slavery is already within every one of her western counties. I have even heard it said that there are more slaves, in proportion to whites, in the northwestern county of Missouri, than within any county of the State. Slavery pressed entirely up to the old western boundary of the State, and when, rather recently, a part of that boundary, at the north-west was moved out a little farther west, slavery followed on quite up to the new line. Now, when the restriction is removed, what is to prevent it from going still further? Climate will not. No peculiarity of the country will—nothing in nature will. Will the disposition of the people prevent it? Those nearest the scene, are all in favor of the extension. The yankees, who are opposed to it may be more numerous; but in military phrase, the battle-field is too far from their base of operations.

But it is said, there now is no law in Nebraska on the subject of slavery; and that, in such case, taking a slave there, operates his freedom. That is good book-law; but is not the rule of actual practice. Wherever slavery is, it has been first introduced without law. The oldest laws we find concerning it, are not laws introducing it; but regulating it, as an already existing thing. A white man takes his slave to Nebraska now; who will inform the negro that he is free? Who will take him before court to test the question of his freedom? In ignorance of his legal emancipation, he is kept chopping, splitting and plowing. Others are brought, and move on in the same track. At last, if ever the time for voting comes, on the question of slavery, the institution already in fact exists in the country, and cannot well be removed. The facts of its presence, and the difficulty of its removal will carry the vote in its favor. Keep it out until a vote is taken, and a vote in favor of it, can not [*sic*] be got in any population of forty thousand, on earth, who have been drawn together by the ordinary motives of emigration and settlement. To get slaves into the country simultaneously with the whites, in the incipient stages of settlement, is the precise stake played for, and won in this Nebraska measure.

The question is asked us, "If slaves will go in, notwithstanding the general principle of law liberates them, why would they not equally go in against positive statute law?—go in, even if the Missouri restriction were maintained?" I answer, because it takes a much bolder man to venture in, with his property, in the latter case, than in the former—because the positive congressional enactment is known to, and respected by all, or nearly all; whereas the negative principle that no law is free law, is not much known except among lawyers. We have some experience of this practical difference. In spite of the Ordinance of '87, a few negroes were brought into Illinois, and held in a state of quasi slavery; not enough, however to carry a vote of the people in favor of the institution when they came to form a constitution. But in the adjoining Missouri country, where there was no ordinance of '87—was no restriction—they were carried ten times, nay a hundred times, as fast, and actually made a slave State. This is fact—naked fact.

Another LULLABY argument is, that taking slaves to new countries does not increase their number—does not make any one slave who otherwise would be free. There is some truth in this, and I am glad of it, but it [is] not WHOLLY true. The African slave trade is not yet effectually suppressed; and if we make a reasonable deduction for the white people amongst us, who are foreigners, and the descendants of foreigners, arriving here since 1808, we shall find the increase of the black population out-running that of the white, to an extent unaccountable, except by supposing that some of them too, have been coming from Africa. If this be so, the opening of new countries to the institution, increases the demand for, and augments the price of slaves, and so does, in fact, make slaves of freemen by causing them to be brought from Africa, and sold into bondage.

But, however this may be, we know the opening of new countries to slavery, tends to the perpetuation of the institution, and so does KEEP men in slavery who otherwise would be free. This result we do not FEEL like favoring, and we are under no legal obligation to suppress our feelings in this respect.

Equal justice to the south, it is said, requires us to consent to the extending of slavery to new countries. That is to say,

Abraham Lincoln—Speech on the Repeal of the Missouri Compromise

inasmuch as you do not object to my taking my hog to Nebraska, therefore I must not object to you taking your slave. Now, I admit this is perfectly logical, if there is no difference between hogs and negroes. But while you thus require me to deny the humanity of the negro, I wish to ask whether you of the south yourselves, have ever been willing to do as much? It is kindly provided that of all those who come into the world, only a small percentage are natural tyrants. That percentage is no larger in the slave States than in the free. The great majority, south as well as north, have human sympathies, of which they can no more divest themselves than they can of their sensibility to physical pain. These sympathies in the bosoms of the southern people, manifest in many ways, their sense of the wrong of slavery, and their consciousness that, after all, there is humanity in the negro. If they deny this, let me address them a few plain questions. In 1820 you joined the north, almost unanimously, in declaring the African slave trade piracy, and in annexing to it the punishment of death. Why did you do this? If you did not feel that it was wrong, why did you join in providing that men should be hung for it? The practice was no more than bringing wild negroes from Africa, to sell to such as would buy them. But you never thought of hanging men for catching and selling wild horses, wild buffaloes or wild bears.

Again, you have amongst you, a sneaking individual, of the class of native tyrants, known as the "SLAVE-DEALER." He watches your necessities, and crawls up to buy your slave, at a speculating price. If you cannot help it, you sell to him; but if you can help it, you drive him from your door. You despise him utterly. You do not recognize him as a friend, or even as an honest man. Your children must not play with his; they may rollick freely with the little negroes, but not with the "slave-dealers" children. If you are obliged to deal with him, you try to get through the job without so much as touching him. It is common with you to join hands with the men you meet; but with the slave dealer you avoid the ceremony—instinctively shrinking from the snaky contact. If he grows rich and retires from business, you still remember him, and still keep up the ban of non-intercourse upon him and his family. Now why is this? You do not so treat the man who deals in corn, cattle or tobacco.

And yet again; there are in the United States and territories, including the District of Columbia, 433,643 free blacks. At $500 per head they are worth over two hundred millions of dollars. How comes this vast amount of property to be running about without owners? We do not see free horses or free cattle running at large. How is this? All these free blacks are the descendants of slaves, or have been slaves themselves, and they would be slaves now, but for SOMETHING which has operated on their white owners, inducing them, at vast pecuniary sacrifices, to liberate them. What is that SOMETHING? Is there any mistaking it? In all these cases it is your sense of justice, and human sympathy, continually telling you, that the poor negro has some natural right to himself—that those who deny it, and make mere merchandise of him, deserve kickings [*sic*], contempt and death.

And now, why will you ask us to deny the humanity of the slave and estimate him only as the equal of the hog? Why ask us to do what you will not do yourselves? Why ask us to do for nothing, what two hundred million of dollars could not induce you to do?

But one great argument in the support of the repeal of the Missouri Compromise, is still to come. That argument is "the sacred right of self-government." It seems our distinguished Senator has found great difficulty in getting his antagonists, even in the Senate to meet him fairly on this argument—some poet has said

"Fools rush in where angels fear to tread."

At the hazard of being thought one of the fools of this quotation, I meet that argument—I rush in, I take that bull by the horns.

I trust I understand, and truly estimate the right of self-government. My faith in the proposition that each man should do precisely as he pleases with all which is exclusively his own, lies at the foundation of the sense of justice there is in me. I extend the principles to communities of men, as well as to individuals. I so extend it, because it is politically wise, as well as naturally just; politically wise, in saving us from broils about matters which do not concern us. Here, or at Washington, I would not trouble myself with the oyster laws of Virginia, or the cranberry laws of Indiana.

The doctrine of self-government is right—absolutely and eternally right—but it has no just application, as here attempted. Or perhaps I should rather say that whether it has such just application depends upon whether a negro is not or is a man. If he is not a man, why in that case, he who is a man may, as a matter of self-government, do just as he pleases with him. But if the negro is a man, is it not to that extent, a total destruction of self-government, to say that he too shall not govern himself? When the white man governs himself that is self-government; but when he governs himself, and also governs another man, that is more than self-government—that is despotism. If the negro is a man, why then my ancient faith teaches me that "all men are created equal;" and that there can be no moral right in connection with one man's making a slave of another.

Judge Douglas frequently, with bitter irony and sarcasm, paraphrases our argument by saying "The white people of Nebraska are good enough to govern themselves, but they are not good enough to govern a few miserable negroes!"

Well I doubt not that the people of Nebraska are, and will continue to be as good as the average of people elsewhere. I do not say the contrary. What I do say is, that no man is good enough to govern another man, without that other's consent. I say this is the leading principle—the sheet anchor of American republicanism. Our Declaration of Independence says: "We hold these truths to be self evident: that all men are created equal; that they are endowed by their Creator with certain inalienable rights; that among these are life, liberty and the pursuit of happiness. That to secure these rights, governments are instituted among men, DERIVING THEIR JUST POWERS FROM THE CONSENT OF THE GOVERNED."

I have quoted so much at this time merely to show that according to our ancient faith, the just powers of governments are derived from the consent of the governed. Now the relation of masters and slaves is, PRO TANTO, a total violation of this principle. The master not only governs the slave without his consent; but he governs him by a set of rules altogether different from those which he prescribes for himself. Allow ALL the governed an equal voice in the government, and that, and that only is self-government.

Let it not be said I am contending for the establishment of political and social equality between the whites and blacks. I have already said the contrary. I am not now combating the argument of NECESSITY, arising from the fact that the blacks are already amongst us; but I am combating what is set up as MORAL argument for allowing them to be taken where they have never yet been—arguing against the EXTENSION of a bad thing, which where it already exists, we must of necessity, manage as we best can.

Abraham Lincoln—Speech on the Repeal of the Missouri Compromise

In support of his application of the doctrine of self-government, Senator Douglas has sought to bring to his aid the opinions and examples of our revolutionary fathers. I am glad he has done this. I love the sentiments of those old-time men; and shall be most happy to abide by their opinions. He shows us that when it was in contemplation for the colonies to break off from Great Britain, and set up a new government for themselves, several of the states instructed their delegates to go for the measure PROVIDED EACH STATE SHOULD BE ALLOWED TO REGULATE ITS DOMESTIC CONCERNS IN ITS OWN WAY. I do not quote; but this in substance. This was right. I see nothing objectionable in it. I also think it probable that it had some reference to the existence of slavery amongst them. I will not deny that it had. But had it, in any reference to the carrying of slavery into NEW COUNTRIES? That is the question; and we will let the fathers themselves answer it.

This same generation of men, and mostly the same individuals of the generation, who declared this principle—who declared independence—who fought the war of the revolution through—who afterwards made the constitution under which we still live—these same men passed the ordinance of '87, declaring that slavery should never go to the north-west territory. I have no doubt Judge Douglas thinks they were very inconsistent in this. It is a question of discrimination between them and him. But there is not an inch of ground left for his claiming that their opinions—their example—their authority—are on his side in this controversy.

Again, is not Nebraska, while a territory, a part of us? Do we not own the country? And if we surrender the control of it, do we not surrender the right of self-government? It is part of ourselves. If you say we shall not control it because it is ONLY part, the same is true of every other part; and when all the parts are gone, what has become of the whole? What is then left of us? What use for the general government, when there is nothing left for it [to] govern?

But you say this question should be left to the people of Nebraska, because they are more particularly interested. If this be the rule, you must leave it to each individual to say for himself whether he will have slaves. What better moral right have thirty-one citizens of Nebraska to say, that the thirty-second shall not hold slaves, than the people of the thirty-one States have to say that slavery shall not go into the thirty-second State at all?

But if it is a sacred right for the people of Nebraska to take and hold slaves there, it is equally their sacred right to buy them where they can buy them cheapest; and that undoubtedly will be on the coast of Africa; provided you will consent to not hang them for going there to buy them. You must remove this restriction too, from the sacred right of self-government. I am aware you say that taking slaves from the States of Nebraska, does not make slaves of freemen; but the African slave-trader can say just as much. He does not catch free negroes and bring them here. He finds them already slaves in the hands of their black captors, and he honestly buys them at the rate of about a red cotton handkerchief a head. This is very cheap, and it is a great abridgement of the sacred right of self-government to hang men for engaging in this profitable trade!

Another important objection to this application of the right of self-government, is that it enables the first FEW, to deprive the succeeding MANY, of a free exercise of the right of self-government. The first few may get slavery IN, and the subsequent many cannot easily get it OUT. How common is the remark now in the slave States—"If we were only clear of our slaves, how much better it would be for us." They are actually deprived of the privilege of governing themselves as they would, by the action of a very few, in the beginning. The same thing was true of the whole nation at the time our constitution was formed.

Whether slavery shall go into Nebraska, or other new territories, is not a matter of exclusive concern to the people who may go there. The whole nation is interested that the best use shall be made of these territories. We want them for the homes of free white people. This they cannot be, to any considerable extent, if slavery shall be planted within them. Slave States are places for poor white people to remove FROM; not to remove TO. New free States are the places for poor people to go to and better their condition. For this use, the nation needs these territories.

Still further; there are constitutional relations between the slave and free States, which are degrading to the latter. We are under legal obligations to catch and return their runaway slaves to them—a sort of dirty, disagreeable job, which I believe, as a general rule the slave-holders will not perform for one another. Then again, in the control of the government—the management of the partnership affairs—they have greatly the advantage of us. By the constitution, each State has two Senators—each has a number of Representatives; in proportion to the number of its people—and each has a number of presidential electors, equal to the whole number of its Senators and Representatives together. But in ascertaining the number of the people, for this purpose, five slaves are counted as being equal to three whites. The slaves do not vote; they are only counted and so used, as to swell the influence of the white people's votes. The practical effect of this is more aptly shown by a comparison of the States of South Carolina and Maine. South Carolina has six representatives, and so has Maine; South Carolina has eight presidential electors, and so has Maine. This is precise equality so far; and, of course they are equal in Senators, each having two. Thus in the control of the government, the two States are equals precisely. But how are they in the number of their white people? Maine has 581,813—while South Carolina has 274,567. Maine has twice as many as South Carolina, and 32,679 over. Thus each white man in South Carolina is more than the double of any man in Maine. This is all because South Carolina, besides her free people, has 384,984 slaves. The South Carolinian has precisely the same advantage over the white man in every other free State, as well as in Maine. He is more than the double of any one of us in this crowd. The same advantage, but not to the same extent, is held by all the citizens of the slave States, over those of the free; and it is an absolute truth, without an exception, that there is no voter in any slave State, but who has more legal power in the government, than any voter in any free State. There is no instance of exact equality; and the disadvantage is against us the whole chapter through. This principle, in the aggregate, gives the slave States, in the present Congress, twenty additional representatives—being seven more than the whole majority by which they passed the Nebraska bill.

Now all this is manifestly unfair; yet I do not mention it to complain of it, in so far as it is already settled. It is in the constitution; and I do not, for that cause, or any other cause, propose to destroy, or alter, or disregard the constitution. I stand to it, fairly, fully, and firmly.

But when I am told I must leave it altogether to OTHER PEOPLE to say whether new partners are to be bred up and brought into the firm, on the same degrading terms against me, I respectfully demur. I insist, that whether I shall be a whole man, or only, the half of one, in comparison with others, is a question in which I am somewhat concerned; and one which no other man can have a sacred right of deciding for me. If I am wrong in this—if it really be a sacred right of self-government, in the man who shall go to Nebraska, to decide whether he will be the EQUAL of me or the DOUBLE of me, then after he shall have exercised that right, and thereby shall have reduced me to a still smaller fraction of a man than I already am, I should like for some gentleman deeply skilled in the mysteries of sacred rights, to provide himself with a microscope, and peep about, and find out, if he can, what has become of my sacred rights! They will surely be too small for detection with the naked eye.

Finally, I insist, that if there is ANY THING which it is the duty of the WHOLE PEOPLE to never entrust to any hands but their own, that thing is the preservation and perpetuity, of their own liberties, and institutions. And if they shall think, as I do, that the extension of slavery endangers them, more than any, or all other causes, how recreant to themselves, if they submit the question, and with it, the fate of their country, to a mere hand-full of men, bent only on temporary self-interest. If this question of slavery extension were an insignificant one— one having no power to do harm—it might be shuffled aside in this way. But being, as it is, the great Behemoth of danger, shall the strong gripe of the nation be loosened upon him, to entrust him to the hands of such feeble keepers?

I have done with this mighty argument, of self-government. Go, sacred thing! Go in peace.

But Nebraska is urged as a great Union-saving measure. Well I too, go for saving the Union. Much as I hate slavery, I would consent to the extension of it rather than see the Union dissolved, just as I would consent to any GREAT evil, to avoid a GREATER one. But when I go to Union saving, I must believe, at least, that the means I employ has some adaptation to the end. To my mind, Nebraska has no such adaptation.

"It hath no relish of salvation in it."

It is an aggravation, rather, of the only one thing which ever endangers the Union. When it came upon us, all was peace and quiet. The nation was looking to the forming of new bonds of Union; and a long course of peace and prosperity seemed to lie before us. In the whole range of possibility, there scarcely appears to me to have been anything, out of which the slavery agitation could have been revived, except the very project of repealing the Missouri compromise. Every inch of territory we owned, already had a definite settlement of the slavery question, and by which, all parties were pledged to abide. Indeed, there was no uninhabited country on the continent, which we could acquire; if we except some extreme northern regions, which are wholly out of the question. In this state of case, the genius of Discord himself, could scarcely have invented a way of again getting [setting?] us by the ears, but by turning back and destroying the peace measures of the past. The councils of that genius seem to have prevailed, the Missouri compromise was repealed; and here we are, in the midst of a new slavery agitation, such, I think, as we have never seen before.

Who is responsible for this? Is it those who resist the measure; or those who, causelessly, brought it forward, and pressed it through, having reason to know, and, in fact, knowing it must and would be so resisted? It could not but be expected by its author, that it would be looked upon as a measure for the extension of slavery, aggravated by a gross breach of faith. Argue as you will, and long as you will, this is the naked FRONT and ASPECT, of the measure. And in this aspect, it could not but produce agitation.

Slavery is founded in the selfishness of man's nature—opposition to it, is [in?] his love of justice. These principles are an eternal antagonism; and when brought into collision so fiercely, as slavery extension brings them, shocks, and throes, and convulsions must ceaselessly follow. Repeal the Missouri compromise—repeal all compromises—repeal the declaration of independence—repeal all past history, you still cannot repeal human nature. It still will be the abundance of man's heart, that slavery extension is wrong; and out of the abundance of his heart, his mouth will continue to speak.

The structure, too, of the Nebraska bill is very peculiar. The people are to decide the question of slavery for themselves; but WHEN they are to decide; or HOW they are to decide; or whether, when the question is once decided, it is to remain so, or is it to be subject to an indefinite succession of new trials, the law does not say, Is it to be decided by the first dozen settlers who arrive there? or is it to await the arrival of a hundred? Is it to be decided by a vote of the people? or a vote of the legislature? or, indeed by a vote of any sort? To these questions, the law gives no answer. There is a mystery about this; for when a member proposed to give the legislature express authority to exclude slavery, it was hooted down by the friends of the bill. This fact is worth remembering. Some yankees, in the east, are sending emigrants to Nebraska, to exclude slavery from it; and, so far as I can judge, they expect the question to be decided by voting, in some way or other. But the Missourians are awake too. They are within a stone's throw of the contested ground. They hold meetings, and pass resolutions, in which not the slightest allusion to voting is made. They resolve that slavery already exists in the territory; that more shall go there; that they, remaining in Missouri will protect it; and that abolitionists shall be hung, or driven away. Through all this, bowie-knives and six-shooters are seen plainly enough; but never a glimpse of the ballot-box. And, really, what is to be the result of this? Each party WITHIN, having numerous and determined backers WITHOUT, is it not probable that the contest will come to blows, and bloodshed? Could there be a more apt invention to bring about collision and violence, on the slavery question, than this Nebraska project is? I do not charge, or believe, that such was intended by Congress; but if they had literally formed a ring, and placed champions within it to fight out the controversy, the fight could be no more likely to come off, than it is. And if this fight should begin, is it likely to take a very peaceful, Union-saving turn? Will not the first drop of blood so shed, be the real knell of the Union?

The Missouri Compromise ought to be restored. For the sake of the Union, it ought to be restored. We ought to elect a House of Representatives which will vote its restoration. If by any means, we omit to do this, what follows? Slavery may or may not be established in Nebraska. But whether it be or not, we shall have repudiated—discarded from the councils of the Nation—the SPIRIT of COMPROMISE; for who after this will ever trust in a national compromise? The spirit of mutual concession—that spirit which first gave us the constitution, and which has thrice saved the Union—we shall have strangled and cast from us forever. And what shall we have in lieu of it? The South flushed with triumph and tempted to excesses; the North, betrayed, as they believe, brooding on wrong and burning for revenge. One side will provoke; the other resent. The one will taunt, the other defy; one agrees [aggresses?], the other retaliates. Already a few in the North, defy all constitutional restraints, resist the execution of the fugitive slave law, and even menace the institution of slavery in the states where it exists.

Already a few in the South, claim the constitutional right to take to and hold slaves in the free states—demand the revival of the slave trade; and demand a treaty with Great Britain by which fugitive slaves may be reclaimed from Canada. As yet they are but few on either side. It is a grave question for the lovers of the Union, whether the final destruction of the Missouri Compromise, and with it the spirit of all compromise will or will not embolden and embitter each of these, and fatally increase the numbers of both.

But restore the compromise, and what then? We thereby restore the national faith, the national confidence, the national feeling of brotherhood. We thereby reinstate the spirit of concession and compromise—that spirit which has never failed us in past perils, and which may be safely trusted for all the future. The south ought to join in doing this. The peace of the nation is as dear to them as to us. In memories of the past and hopes of the future, they share as largely as we. It would be on their part, a great act—great in its spirit, and great in its effect. It would be worth to the nation a hundred years' purchase of peace and prosperity. And what of sacrifice would they make? They only surrender to us, what they gave us for a consideration long, long ago; what they have not now, asked for, struggled or cared for; what has been thrust upon them, not less to their own astonishment than to ours.

But it is said we cannot restore it; that though we elect every member of the lower house, the Senate is still against us. It is quite true, that of the Senators who passed the Nebraska bill, a majority of the whole Senate will retain their seats in spite of the elections of this and the next year. But if at these elections, their several constituencies shall clearly express their will against Nebraska, will these senators disregard their will? Will they neither obey, nor make room for those who will?

But even if we fail to technically restore the compromise, it is still a great point to carry a popular vote in favor of the restoration. The moral weight of such a vote can not [sic] be estimated too highly. The authors of Nebraska are not at all satisfied with the destruction of the compromise—an endorsement of this PRINCIPLE, they proclaim to be the great object. With them, Nebraska alone is a small matter—to establish a principle, for FUTURE USE, is what they particularly desire.

That future use is to be the planting of slavery wherever in the wide world, local and unorganized opposition cannot prevent it. Now if you wish to give them this endorsement—if you wish to establish this principle—do so. I shall regret it; but it is your right. On the contrary if you are opposed to the principle—intend to give it no such endorsement—let no wheedling, no sophistry, divert you from throwing a direct vote against it.

Some men, mostly whigs, who condemn the repeal of the Missouri Compromise, nevertheless hesitate to go for its restoration, lest they be thrown in company with the abolitionist. Will they allow me as an old whig to tell them good humoredly [sic], that I think this is very silly? Stand with anybody that stands RIGHT. Stand with him while he is right and PART with him when he goes wrong. Stand WITH the abolitionist in restoring the Missouri Compromise; and stand AGAINST him when he attempts to repeal the fugitive slave law. In the latter case you stand with the southern disunionist [*sic*]. What of that you are still right. In both cases you are right. In both cases you oppose [expose?] the dangerous extremes. In both you stand on middle ground and hold the ship level and steady. In both you are national and nothing less than national. This is good old whig ground. To desert such ground, because of any company, is to be less than a whig—less than a man—less than an American.

I particularly object to the NEW position which the avowed principle of this Nebraska law gives to slavery in the body politic. I object to it because it assumes that there CAN be MORAL RIGHT in the enslaving of one man by another. I object to it as a dangerous dalliance for a few [free?] people—a sad evidence that, feeling prosperity we forget right—that liberty, as a principle, we have ceased to revere. I object to it because the fathers of the republic eschewed, and rejected it. The argument of "Necessity" was the only argument they ever admitted in favor of slavery; and so far, and so far only as it carried them, did they ever go. They found the institution existing among us, which they could not help; and they cast blame upon the British King for having permitted its introduction. BEFORE the constitution, they prohibited its introduction into the north-western Territory—the only country we owned, then free from it. AT the framing and adoption of the constitution, they forbore to so much as mention the word "slave" or "slavery" in the whole instrument. In the provision for the recovery of fugitives, the slave is spoken of as a "PERSON HELD TO SERVICE OR LABOR." In that prohibiting the abolition of the African slave trade for twenty years, that trade is spoken of as "The migration or importation of such persons as any of the States NOW EXISTING, shall think proper to admit," &c. These are the only provisions alluding to slavery. Thus, the thing is hid away, in the constitution, just as an afflicted man hides away a wen or a cancer, which he dares not cut out at once, lest he bleed to death; with the promise, nevertheless, that the cutting may begin at the end of a given time. Less than this our fathers COULD not do; and NOW [MORE?] they WOULD not do. Necessity drove them so far, and farther, they would not go. But this is not all. The earliest Congress, under the constitution, took the same view of slavery. They hedged and hemmed it in to the narrowest limits of necessity.

In 1794, they prohibited an out-going slave-trade—that is, the taking of slaves FROM the United States to sell. In 1798, they prohibited the bringing of slaves from Africa, INTO the Mississippi Territory—this territory then comprising what are now the States of Mississippi and Alabama. This was TEN YEARS before they had the authority to do the same thing as to the States existing at the adoption of the constitution.

In 1800 they prohibited AMERICAN CITIZENS from trading in slaves between foreign countries—as, for instance, from Africa to Brazil.

In 1803 they passed a law in aid of one or two State laws, in restraint of the internal slave trade.

In 1807, in apparent hot haste, they passed the law, nearly a year in advance to take effect the first day of 1808—the very first day the constitution would permit—prohibiting the African slave trade by heavy pecuniary and corporal penalties.

In 1820, finding these provisions ineffectual, they declared the trade piracy, and annexed to it, the extreme penalty of death.

While all this was passing in the general government, five or six of the original slave States had adopted systems of gradual emancipation; and by which the institution was rapidly becoming extinct within these limits.

Thus we see, the plain unmistakable spirit of that age, towards slavery, was hostility to the PRINCIPLE, and toleration, ONLY BY NECESSITY.

But NOW it is to be transformed into a "sacred right." Nebraska brings it forth, places it on the high road to extension and perpetuity; and, with a pat on its back, says to it, "Go, and God speed you." Henceforth it is to be the chief jewel of the nation—the very figure-head of the ship of State. Little by little, but steadily as man's march to the grave, we have been giving up the OLD for the NEW faith. Near eighty years ago we began by declaring that all men are created equal; but now from that beginning we have run down to the other declaration, that for SOME men to enslave OTHERS is a "sacred right of self-government." These principles can not [sic] stand together. They are as opposite as God and mammon; and whoever holds to the one, must despise the other. When Pettit, in connection with his support of the Nebraska bill, called the Declaration of Independence "a self-evident lie" he only did what consistency and candor require all other Nebraska men to do. Of the forty odd Nebraska Senators who sat present and heard him, no one rebuked him. Nor am I apprized that any Nebraska newspaper, or any Nebraska orator, in the whole nation, has ever yet rebuked him. If this had been said among Marion's men, Southerners though they were, what would have become of the man who said it? If this had been said to the men who captured Andre, the man who said it, would probably have been hung sooner than Andre was. If it had been said in old Independence Hall, seventy-eight years ago, the very door-keeper would have throttled the man, and thrust him into the street.

Let no one be deceived. The spirit of seventy-six and the spirit of Nebraska, are utter antagonisms; and the former is being rapidly displaced by the latter.

Fellow countrymen—Americans south, as well as north, shall we make no effort to arrest this? Already the liberal party throughout the world, express the apprehension "that the one retrograde institution in America, is undermining the principles of progress, and fatally violating the noblest political system the world ever saw." This is not the taunt of enemies, but the warning of friends. Is it quite safe to disregard it—to despise it? Is there no danger to liberty itself, in discarding the earliest practice, and first precept of our ancient faith? In our greedy chase to make profit of the negro, let us beware, lest we "cancel and tear to pieces" even the white man's charter of freedom.

Our republican robe is soiled, and trailed in the dust. Let us repurify [sic] it. Let us turn and wash it white, in the spirit, if not the blood, of the Revolution. Let us turn slavery from its claims of "moral right," back upon its existing legal rights, and its arguments of "necessity." Let us return it to the position our fathers gave it; and there let it rest in peace. Let us re-adopt the Declaration of Independence, and with it, the practices, and policy, which harmonize with it. Let north and south—let all Americans—let all lovers of liberty everywhere—join in the great and good work. If we do this, we shall not only have saved the Union; but we shall have so saved it, as to make, and to keep it, forever worthy of the saving. We shall have so saved it, that the succeeding millions of free happy people, the world over, shall rise up, and call us blessed, to the latest generations.

At Springfield, twelve days ago, where I had spoken substantially as I have here, Judge Douglas replied to me—and as he is to reply to me here, I shall attempt to anticipate him, by noticing some of the points he made there. He commenced by stating I had assumed all the way through, that the principle of the Nebraska bill, would have the effect of extending slavery. He denied that this was INTENDED, or that this EFFECT would follow.

I will not re-open the argument upon this point. That such was the intention, the world believed at the start, and will continue to believe. This was the COUNTENANCE of the thing; and, both friends and enemies, instantly recognized it as such. That countenance cannot now be changed by argument. You can as easily argue the color out of the negroes' skin. Like the "bloody hand" you may wash it, and wash it, the red witness of guilt still sticks, and stares horribly at you.

Next he says, congressional intervention never prevented slavery, anywhere—that it did not prevent it in the north west territory, now [nor?] in Illinois—that in fact, Illinois came into the Union as a slave State—that the principle of the Nebraska bill expelled it from Illinois, from several old States, from everywhere.

Now this is mere quibbling all the way through. If the ordinance of '87 did not keep slavery out of the north west territory, how happens it that the north west shore of the Ohio river is entirely free from it; while the south east shore, less than a mile distant, along nearly the whole length of the river, is entirely covered with it?

If that ordinance did not keep it out of Illinois, what was it that made the difference between Illinois and Missouri? They lie side by side, the Mississippi river only dividing them; while their early settlements were within the same latitude. Between 1810 and 1820 the number of slaves in Missouri INCREASED 7,211; while in Illinois, in the same ten years, they DECREASED 51. This appears by the census returns. During nearly all of that ten years, both were territories—not States. During this time, the ordinance forbid slavery to go into Illinois; and NOTHING forbid it to go into Missouri. It DID go into Missouri, and did NOT go into Illinois. That is the fact. Can anyone doubt as to the reason of it?

But, he says, Illinois came into the Union as a slave State. Silence, perhaps, would be the best answer to this flat contradiction of the known history of the country. What are the facts upon which this bold assertion is based? When we first acquired the country, as far back as 1787, there were some slaves within it, held by the French inhabitants at Kaskaskia. The territorial legislation, admitted a few negroes, from the slave States, as indentured servants. One year after the adoption of the first State constitution the whole number of them was—what do you think? just 117—while the aggregate free population was 55,094—about 470 to one. Upon this state of facts, the people framed their constitution prohibiting the further introduction of slavery, with a sort of guaranty to the owners of the few indentured servants, giving freedom to their children to be born thereafter, and making no mention whatever, of any supposed slave for life. Out of this small matter, the Judge manufactures his argument that Illinois came into the Union as a slave State. Let the facts be the answer to the argument.

The principles of the Nebraska bill, he says, expelled slavery from Illinois? The principle of that bill first planted it here—that is, it first came, because there was no law to prevent it—first came before we owned the country; and finding it here, and having the ordinance of '87 to prevent its increasing, our people struggled along, and finally got rid of it as best they could.

But the principle of the Nebraska bill abolished slavery in several of the old States. Well, it is true that several of the old States, in the last quarter of the last century, did adopt systems of gradual emancipation, by which the institution has finally become extinct within their limits; but it MAY or MAY NOT be true that the principle of the Nebraska bill was the cause that led to the adoption of these measures. It is now more than fifty years, since the last of these States adopted its system of emancipation. If Nebraska bill is the real author of these benevolent works, it is rather deplorable, that he has, for so long a time, ceased working all together. Is there not some reason to suspect that it was the principle of the REVOLUTION, and not the principle of Nebraska bill, that led to emancipation in these old States? Leave it to the people of those old emancipating States, and I am quite sure they will decide, that neither that, nor any other good thing, ever did, or ever will come of Nebraska bill.

In the course of my main argument, Judge Douglas interrupted me to say, that the principle [of] the Nebraska bill was very old; that it originated when God made man and placed good and evil before him, allowing him to choose for himself, being responsible for the choice he should make. At the time I thought this was merely playful; and I answered it accordingly. But in his reply to me he renewed it, as a serious argument. In seriousness then, the facts of this proposition are not true as stated. God did not place good and evil before man, telling him to make his choice. On the contrary, he did tell him there was one tree, of the fruit of which, he should not eat, upon pain of certain death. I should scarcely wish so strong a prohibition against slavery in Nebraska.

But this argument strikes me as not a little remarkable in another particular—in its strong resemblance to the old argument for the "Divine right of Kings." By the latter, the King is to do just as he pleases with his white subjects, being responsible to God alone. By the former the white man is to do just as he pleases with his black slaves, being responsible to God alone. The two things are precisely alike; and it is but natural that they should find similar arguments to sustain them.

I had argued, that the application of the principle of self-government, as contended for, would require the revival of the African slave trade—that no argument could be made in favor of a man's right to take slaves to Nebraska, which could not be equally well made in favor of his right to bring them from the coast of Africa. The Judge replied, that the constitution requires the suppression of the foreign slave trade; but does not require the prohibition of slavery in the territories. That is a mistake, in point of fact. The constitution does NOT require the action of Congress in either case; and it does AUTHORIZE it in both. And so, there is still no difference between the cases.

In regard to what I had said, the advantage the slave States have over the free, in the matter of representation, the Judge replied that we, in the free States, count five free negroes as five white people, while in the slave States, they count five slaves as three whites only; and that the advantage, at last, was on the side of the free States.

Now, in the slave States, they count free negroes just as we do; and it so happens that besides their slaves, they have as many free negroes as we have, and thirty-three thousand over. Thus their free negroes more than balance ours; and their advantage over us, in consequence of their slaves, still remains as I stated it.

In reply to my argument, that the compromise measures of 1850, were a system of equivalents; and that the provisions of no one of them could fairly be carried to other subjects, without its corresponding equivalent being carried with it, the Judge denied out-right, that these measures had any connection with, or dependence upon, each other. This is mere desperation. If they have no connection, why are they always spoken of in connection? Why has he so spoken of them, a thousand times? Why has he constantly called them a SERIES of measures? Why does everybody call them a compromise? Why was California kept out of the Union, six or seven months, if it was not because of its connection with the other measures? Webster's leading definition of the verb "to compromise" is "to adjust and settle a difference, by mutual agreement with concessions of claims by the parties." This conveys precisely the popular understanding of the word compromise. We knew, before the Judge told us, that these measures passed separately, and in distinct bills; and that no two of them were passed by the votes of precisely the same members. But we also know, and so does he know, that no one of them could have passed both branches of Congress but for the understanding that the others were to pass also. Upon this understanding each got votes, which it could have got in no other way. It is this fact, that gives to the measures their true character; and it is the universal knowledge of this fact, that has given them the name of compromise so expressive of that true character.

I had asked "If in carrying the provisions of the Utah and New Mexico laws to Nebraska, you could clear away other objection, how can you leave Nebraska 'perfectly free' to introduce slavery BEFORE she forms a constitution—during her territorial government?—while the Utah and New Mexico laws only authorize it WHEN they form constitutions, and are admitted into the Union?" To this Judge Douglas answered that the Utah and New Mexico laws, also authorized it BEFORE; and to prove this, he read from one of their laws, as follows: "That the legislative power of said territory shall extend to all rightful subjects of legislation consistent with the constitution of the United States and the provisions of this act."

Now it is perceived from the reading of this, that there is nothing express upon the subject; but that the authority is sought to be implied merely, for the general provision of "all rightful subjects of legislation." In reply to this, I insist, as a legal rule of construction, as well as the plain popular view of the matter, that the EXPRESS provision for Utah and New Mexico coming in with slavery if they choose, when they shall form constitutions, is an EXCLUSION of all implied authority on the same subject—that Congress, having the subject distinctly in their minds, when they made the express provision, they therein expressed their WHOLE meaning on that subject.

The Judge rather insinuated that I had found it convenient to forget the Washington territorial law passed in 1853. This was a division of Oregon, organizing the northern part, as the territory of Washington. He asserted that, by this act, the ordinance of '87 theretofore existing in Oregon, was repealed;

that nearly all the members of Congress voted for it, beginning in the H.R., with Charles Allen of Massachusetts, and ending with Richard Yates, of Illinois; and that he could not understand how those who now oppose the Nebraska bill, so voted then, unless it was because it was then too soon after both the great political parties had ratified the compromises of 1850, and the ratification therefore too fresh, to be then repudiated.

Now I had seen the Washington act before; and I have carefully examined it since; and I aver that there is no repeal of the ordinance of '87, or of any prohibition of slavery, in it. In express terms, there is absolutely nothing in the whole law upon the subject—in fact, nothing to lead a reader to THINK of the subject. To my judgment, it is equally free from everything from which such repeal can be legally implied; but however this may be, are men now to be entrapped by a legal implication, extracted from covert language, introduced perhaps, for the very purpose of entrapping them? I sincerely wish every man could read this law quite through, carefully watching every sentence, and every line, for a repeal of the ordinance of '87 or anything equivalent to it.

Another point on the Washington act. If it was intended to be modeled after the Utah and New Mexico acts, as Judge

Douglas, insists, why was it not inserted in it, as in them, that Washington was to come in with or without slavery as she may choose at the adoption of her constitution? It has no such provision in it; and I defy the ingenuity of man to give a reason for the omission, other than that it was not intended to follow the Utah and New Mexico laws in regard to the question of slavery.

The Washington act not only differs vitally from the Utah and New Mexico acts; but the Nebraska act differs vitally from both. By the latter act the people are left "perfectly free" to regulate their own domestic concerns, &c.; but in all the former, all their laws are to be submitted to Congress, and if disapproved are to be null. The Washington act goes even further; it absolutely prohibits the territorial legislation [legislature?], by very strong and guarded language, from establishing banks, or borrowing money on the faith of the territory. Is this the sacred right of self-government we hear vaunted so much? No sir, the Nebraska bill finds no model in the acts of '50 or the Washington act. It finds no model in any law from Adam till today. As Phillips says of Napoleon, the Nebraska act is grand, gloomy, and peculiar; wrapped in the solitude of its own originality; without a model, and without a shadow upon the earth.

In the course of his reply, Senator Douglas remarked, in substance, that he had always considered this government was made for the white people and not for the negroes. Why, in point of mere fact, I think so too. But in this remark of the Judge, there is a significance, which I think is the key to the great mistake (if there is any such mistake) which he has made in this Nebraska measure. It shows that the Judge has no very vivid impression that the negro is a human; and consequently has no idea that there can be any moral question in legislating about him. In his view, the question of whether a new country shall be slave or free, is a matter of as utter indifference, as it is whether his neighbor shall plant his farm with tobacco, or stock it with horned cattle. Now, whether this view is right or wrong, it is very certain that the great mass of mankind take a totally different view. They consider slavery a great moral wrong; and their feelings against it, is not evanescent, but eternal. It lies at the very foundation of their sense of justice; and it cannot be trifled with. It is a great and durable element of popular action, and, I think, no statesman can safely disregard it.

Our Senator also objects that those who oppose him in this measure do not entirely agree with one another. He reminds me that in my firm adherence to the constitutional rights of the slave States, I differ widely from others who are co-operating with me in opposing the Nebraska bill; and he says it is not quite fair to oppose him in this variety of ways. He should remember that he took us by surprise—astounded us—by this measure. We were thunderstruck and stunned; and we reeled and fell in utter confusion. But we rose each fighting, grasping whatever he could first reach—a scythe—a pitchfork—a chopping axe, or a butcher's cleaver. We struck in the direction of the sound; and we are rapidly closing in upon him. He must not think to divert us from our purpose, by showing us that our drill, our dress, and our weapons, are not entirely perfect and uniform. When the storm shall be past, he shall find us still Americans; no less devoted to the continued Union and prosperity of the country than heretofore.

Finally, the Judge invokes against me, the memory of Clay and of Webster. They were great men; and men of great deeds. But where have I assailed them? For what is it, that their life-long enemy, shall now make profit, by assuming to defend them against me, their life-long friend? I go against the repeal of the

Abraham Lincoln—Speech on the Repeal of the Missouri Compromise

Missouri compromise; did they ever go for it? They went for the compromise of 1850; did I ever go against them? They were greatly devoted to the Union; to the small measure of my ability, was I ever less so? Clay and Webster were dead before this question arose; by what authority shall our Senator say they would espouse his side of it, if alive? Mr. Clay was the leading spirit in making the Missouri compromise; is it very credible that if now alive, he would take the lead in the breaking of it? The truth is that some support from whigs is now a necessity with the Judge, and for thus it is, that the names of Clay and Webster are now invoked. His old friends have deserted him in such numbers as to leave too few to live by. He came to his own, and his own received him not, and Lo! he turns unto the Gentiles.

A word now as to the Judge's desperate assumption that the compromises of '50 had no connection with one another; that Illinois came into the Union as a slave state, and some other similar ones. This is no other than a bold denial of the history of the country. If we do not know that the Compromises of '50 were dependent on each other; if we do not know that Illinois came into the Union as a free state—we do not know anything. If we do not know these things, we do not know that we ever had a revolutionary war, or such a chief as Washington. To deny these things is to deny our national axioms, or dogmas, at least; and it puts an end to all argument. If a man will stand up and assert, and repeat, and re-assert, that two and two do not make four, I know nothing in the power of argument that can stop him. I think I can answer the Judge so long as he sticks to the premises; but when he flies from them, I cannot work an argument into the consistency of a maternal gag, and actually close his mouth with it. In such a case I can only commend him to the seventy thousand answers just in from Pennsylvania, Ohio and Indiana.

Address Delivered at the Dedication of the Cemetery at Gettysburg
Abraham Lincoln
November 19, 1863

Fourscore and seven years ago our fathers brought forth on this continent, a new nation, conceived in Liberty, and dedicated to the proposition that all men are created equal.

Abraham Lincoln—Address Delivered at the Dedication of the Cemetery at Gettysburg

Now we are engaged in a great civil war, testing whether that nation, or any nation so conceived and so dedicated, can long endure. We are met on a great battlefield of that war. We have come to dedicate a portion of that field, as a final resting place for those who here gave their lives that that nation might live. It is altogether fitting and proper that we should do this.

But, in a larger sense, we cannot dedicate—we cannot consecrate—we cannot hallow—this ground. The brave men, living and dead, who struggled here, have consecrated it, far above our poor power to add or detract. The world will little note, nor long remember what we say here, but it can never forget what they did here. It is for us the living, rather, to be dedicated here to the unfinished work which they who fought here have thus far so nobly advanced. It is rather for us to be here dedicated to the great task remaining before us—that from these honored dead we take increased devotion to that cause for which they gave the last full measure of devotion— that we here highly resolve that these dead shall not have died in vain— that this nation, under God, shall have a new birth of freedom—and that government of the people, by the people, for the people, shall not perish from the earth.

Second Inaugural Address
Abraham Lincoln
March 4, 1865
Washington, D.C.

<u>Fellow Countrymen</u>

At this second appearing to take the oath of the Presidential office, there is less occasion for an extended address than there was at the first. Then a statement, somewhat in detail, of a course to be pursued, seemed fitting and proper. Now, at the expiration of four years, during which public declarations have been constantly called forth on every point and phase of the great contest which still absorbs the attention, and engrosses the energies of the nation, little that is new could be presented. The progress of our arms, upon which all else chiefly depends, is as well known to the public as to myself; and it is, I trust, reasonably satisfactory and encouraging to all. With high hope for the future, no prediction in regard to it is ventured.

One eighth of the whole population were colored slaves, not distributed generally over the Union, but localized in the Southern part of it. These slaves constituted a peculiar and powerful interest. All knew that this interest was, somehow, the cause of the war. To strengthen, perpetuate, and extend this interest was the object for which the insurgents would rend the Union, even by war; while the government claimed no right to do more than to restrict the territorial enlargement of it. Neither party expected for the war, the magnitude, or the duration, which it has already attained. Neither anticipated that the <u>cause</u> of the conflict might cease with, or even before, the conflict itself should cease. Each looked for an easier triumph, and a result less fundamental and astounding. Both read the same Bible, and pray to the same God; and each invokes His aid against the other. It may seem strange that any men should dare to ask a just God's assistance in wringing their bread from the sweat of other men's faces; but let us judge not that we be not judged. The prayers of both could not be answered; that of neither has been answered fully. The Almighty has His own purposes. "Woe unto the world because of offences! for it must needs be that offences come; but woe to that man by whom the offence cometh!" If we shall suppose that American Slavery is one of those offences which, in the providence of God, must needs come, but which, having continued through His appointed time, He now wills to remove, and that He gives to both North and South, this terrible war as the woe due to those by whom the offence came, shall we discern therein any departure from those divine attributes which the believers in a Living God always ascribe to Him? Fondly do we hope—fervently do we pray—that this mighty scourge of war may speedily pass away. Yet, if God wills that it continue, until all the wealth piled by the bond-man's two hundred and fifty years of unrequited toil shall be sunk, and until every drop of blood drawn with the lash, shall be paid by another drawn with the sword, as was said three thousand years ago, so still it must be said "the judgments of the Lord, are true and righteous altogether."

Abraham Lincoln—Second Inaugural Address

With malice toward none; with charity for all; with firmness in the right, as God gives us to see the right, let us strive on to finish the work we are in; to bind up the nation's wounds; to care for him who shall have borne the battle, and for his widow, and his orphan—to do all which may achieve and cherish a just, and a lasting peace, among ourselves, and with all nations.

Final Thoughts

Leadership is not easy. It is costly. It sometimes hurts. It is often lonely but never alone. When leadership is done from right motives and through uplifting methods of people motivation, it works. In fact, under these conditions, it always works. And it's always hard.

I am struck by the knowledge that some people truly believe that leadership "just happens" or that it is personality-driven or follows a list of inherent traits that if you have them you're a leader, and if you don't, well, you're not a leader and never will be. "Too bad—you don't qualify."

These versions or styles of leadership at some level miss the central point: leadership is a *decision* about the success of someone else. And sometimes those decisions are highly unpopular. Often they include sacrifice and sometimes those sacrifices are immense.

Regardless, if you make a decision to help someone else succeed by helping create opportunity for success and contributions at greater levels than you, and if you change your behaviors though this change may be uncomfortable or challenging to make your desires for someone else's success come true through your teaching, modeling, encouragement, and support, then you are a leader and probably a pretty good one. How much do you want to lead like this?

If you want to lead like this in any environment, and you truly have the benefit of your followers at the core of your motivation, you will consider following Lincoln's example. He invested all he could for the success of his cause and the benefit of all his "followers"—the people of the United States—in perpetuity.

Leadership is not simplistic, but at its core it is simple. It's all about wanting another's success, making a decision about their success, and changing your behaviors to help your desire to contribute the framework for their success to become reality.

We've covered it—the truth is iron-clad. The only remaining consideration is whether you want to become a leader like this and achieve the success in your environment like Lincoln achieved in his, no matter the cost. If you truly desire to be a leader like that, then begin by changing your behaviors. Even in doing that your leadership will be shown. Results are sure over time. Build for what you want and will be shown to endure. Generations of people who follow you will be grateful because they just might be part of the legacy you have created.

Acknowledgements

Down through the years I have enjoyed many conversations with individuals who have told me that they wanted to play the piano like I do and many who have said that they wanted to write a book like I have done. I tell them I appreciate their compliment and their confidence (and I do), and I tell them I applaud their desires—not necessarily their expressions to be "like" me or to do something I have done—rather, I applaud their words that express the desires of their hearts. Those expressions are the points where the challenge of initiating action becomes the defining moment, the make or break option which determines if desire will move down the road toward fulfillment of a dream.

As you would well imagine, very few people who have made statements like that to me have actually done anything about what they said their hopes, dreams, and desires were. There is no judgment here; it's just fact. And those facts speak for themselves.

In conversations like the ones above, I can usually sense some degree of commitment if a commitment to achieve is present. Many times it is. If appropriate, I will ask the individual if they are willing to work as hard as I have, or I will ask them when they plan to start taking lessons, or write their book. My questions to them do not represent attitudes or actions of arrogance on my part; I am simply ascertaining whether or not the person with whom I am talking is really serious about what they say they want to do. While in the final analysis most are not, thankfully some are. Those are the people it becomes a unique privilege to encourage and help in whatever ways are mutually deemed best.

When someone really wants to achieve, the bottom line truth is that hard work follows their dream and any conversation about it. Work is not an option; it's a requirement. I am sure there are many reasons why a person will not put action toward the fulfillment of an expressed desire, but one that must be considered often is fear: fear of failure, or even fear of success. This kind of fear usually comes from the recognition and evaluation of perceived and real risk as well as the costs involved in moving beyond the status quo. Those costs certainly encompass time, energy, money, and other resources that many people may not have the desire to spend.

Risk is simply a part of reaching out beyond a comfort zone to accomplish something greater than what we have now. Usually the degree of reasonable risk and the costs required are indelibly tied to a degree of opportunity for responsibly earned reward.

Where risk is not willingly assumed by people who *say* they want to move forward, generally nothing of significance will happen. The key word here is *willingly*. Pushing them doesn't work, coercion backfires, hoping against hope that someone will venture out is fruitless, encouragement offered to someone who is not convinced within themselves that they can or even want to move forward is wasted energy, and investing in a person like this comes up empty handed in terms of any return on investment. Here's the reason these actions *don't* produce beneficial results: the person with the dream for success does not *own the responsibility* of fulfilling that dream.

When in this book you read that the leader's job is to make decisions about someone else's success you may have seen the importance of the word *about*. The leader cannot and must not try to own the success of another because it can't be done. Making a decision *about* another's success means that the leader appreciates and validates the goal and then helps the follower achieve the goal by offering and often providing "teaching, modeling, encouragement, and support."

A person of determination, a responsible individual, one with earnest desire and a desire to work recognizes that building upon those actions from committed leaders often constructs the road to achievement. A dedicated individual also recognizes that talents are truly gifts from God and that gratitude for them and the opportunities they may present is right. That person knows that one of the greatest ways of expressing gratitude to God for the gifts from God is to fully develop and contribute the talents that have entrusted by God to him or her.

Further, that person knows that *apart from hard work those talents will remain dormant and expressionless at worst, or mediocre and not exceptional at best*, and that *any government, "village", even family and friends can never be deemed to be or thought of as the ones who "arrange for" and somehow "guarantee" success*. In the final analysis

success is up to the person, not his or her environment. You, the individual, build what you truly want—no one else does.

Lincoln was a backwoodsman who became President. He had little support from his family and according to his own recollection, the total amount of his formal education, in aggregate, amounted to less than one year. How did he do it? He worked hard, very hard. Although he was often disappointed, *he never gave up*. He worked hard because he knew that if he didn't, no one else would do it for him.

In America we are blessed with a government structure that promotes achievement, according to the founding documents. The government's job is primarily to protect the inalienable rights of the individual, those declared in the Declaration of Independence to be "Life, Liberty and the pursuit of Happiness." In fact, according to that same document, it's the primary reason government exists, or at least the reason that this government was formed.

Government's job is *not* to assure economic fairness or to level the playing field between those who have the capability to work hard and do it, and those who have the capability and don't. Compassion is never seen in enabling where assistance creates dependence on government. Compassion is better seen in bold empowerment where drive and determination create independence and eventually interdependence where people work together to achieve mutually desired goals.

Achievers have the responsibility to maximize personal gifting and talents because they recognize unlimited opportunities for business and personal success. They also know that as they achieve their goals they have a responsibility to invest in others. According to Luke 12:48b (NIV): "From everyone who has been given much, much will be demanded; and from the one who has been entrusted with much, much more will be asked." Investment in others who want to do likewise is part of what achievers can and should do.

Achievement comes before investment. Remember, you can't give away something you don't have. *You* must become who you need to become in order to be able to help someone else accomplish their goals. If you are given or create the option to invest in another person, do it but only if they want it and want to work hard for it.

I want to acknowledge Lincoln. He was a pioneer who pointed up and followed the ways of American opportunity, who demonstrated in real life that America works as long as he did. I want to acknowledge his leadership that demonstrated the enduring effects that leadership based on right principles will produce. I also want to acknowledge his dependence upon God that matured over time.

Further, I want to acknowledge you, the reader, to be a person of investigation of the principled truths of freedom, opportunity, hard work, leadership, investment, and responsibility. If you want success, consider the changes you must make to incorporate those principles into your practice of leadership. In short, if you want success, lead like this.

There are no guarantees of success, and there shouldn't be. What we have, given by God, is opportunity. In America because of great sacrifice of those who have gone before us, we have the options to turn opportunity into reality. You have to make the most of these possibilities as a follower, leader, investor, and responsible individual. Be encouraged in your efforts.

Products and Services

The products and services offered by the Glen Aubrey for-profit companies can be accessed through this website: www.glenaubrey.com. Three organizations listed on this website are:

1. Creative Team Resources Group (CTRG), www.ctrg.com. CTRG is a full-service team training and management consulting organization serving thousands of people in organizations in the private and public sectors since 1998.
2. Creative Team Publishing (CTP), a division of CTRG, www.CreativeTeamPublishing.com. CTP is a fee-for service publisher. The firm was started in 2007 to

publish and distribute books of business development, leadership training, inspiration, insight, human achievement, and positive general interest.

3. Creative Music Enterprises (CME), a creative arts production firm, www.CreativeMusicEnterprises.com. This organization has served thousands of clients with music and creative productions of virtually all kinds since 1976. Services offered include performance, production, promotion, and publication of individual, commercial, and professional clients' works.

A fourth organization is dedicated to serving non-profit entities. This is Creative Ministry Teams, Inc. (CMT), www.CreativeMinistryTeams.org. Creative Ministry Teams is a 501 (c) (3) organization and was begun in 1999.

You are invited to access these organizations through their websites, or through **www.glenaubrey.com**.

www.ingramcontent.com/pod-product-compliance
Lightning Source LLC
Chambersburg PA
CBHW022036290426
44109CB00014B/876